The Goldfinch

by

Donna Tartt

in

A Brief Read

(A Summary)

by

Tara Waller

Table of Contents

A Brief Read

Do you love to read, but don't have the time? Do you wish you could read every book on the best sellers list? Can you afford every book on the best sellers list?

The A Brief Read series is for you! Every year, over two million books are published, but there is never enough time and money to read them all.

Each A Brief Read book is approximately 25 to 35% of the length of the original book. Our writers strive to retain the story line, suspense, and overall feel of the original book, but you can read it in a quarter of the time! You will recognize A Brief Read Summaries by their well developed characters and quick pace.

If you enjoy the story, you might even work in some time to read the original. If there's a book that you'd like to see in A Brief Read, let us know!

Visit us on Amazon or ABriefRead.com!

Like us on Facebook for special promotions!

About the Author

A Greenwood, Mississippi native, Donna Tartt was born on December 23, 1963. She began her writing career as a freshman at the University of Mississippi. She was encouraged to pursue her writing and decided to follow this dream. In 1982, she surrounded herself with other literary scholars after transferring to Bennington College.

In 1992, Tartt published her first novel, *The Secret History,* which received a lot of attention. Ten years later, in 2002, she released *The Little Friend.* For this one, she was awarded the 2003 WH Smith Literary Award. *The Goldfinch* is her third novel, released on October 22, 2013. Like the other two, it has attracted praise and new fans with ease. Between novels, Donna Tartt remains involved in a number of writing projects.

Introduction

The Goldfinch by Donna Tartt centers on the presence of Carel Fabritius' painting in the life of a young boy named Theodore Decker and those around him. Young Theo survives a traumatic explosion in a New York City museum, in which he lost his mother. He struggles with grief, being displaced to his father's new life in Vegas and surviving early adolescence with the influence of drugs and alcohol. The loss of his mother is not the only death which poor Theo will suffer, and he eventually returns to the City, coming into his own as young man.

Throughout, the presence of Fabritius' simple painting of a goldfinch remains an unchanging force in Theo's life. Donna Tartt combines techniques reminiscent of J.D. Salinger, the contemporary effects of a thriller and the classical themes of Fyodor Dostoevsky to create a complex yet heart-wrenching story of a young boy surviving the ups and downs of a difficult life.

The Goldfinch by Carel Fabritius

Part One

The absurd does not liberate; it binds. – Albert Camus

Chapter One: The Boy Who Survived

1

Having left New York quickly, I was in Amsterdam when I started having dreams about my mother again. It had been years since that had happened. It was Christmas time in Amsterdam with a lot of activity going on outside. I hadn't yet gone out to explore the city. I was a bit preoccupied with other things on my mind, so I kept to myself and stayed indoors most of the time.

Before there were many people milling about, I would go down to grab the newspaper and then head back to my room to scan the headlines. The Dutch news had it all over, but the others weren't as concerned. I didn't know if anyone knew who I was or not. I was cold because I hadn't brought the right clothes with me, so I would spend a lot of time drifting in and out of sleep, staying in bed most of the day. I would worry about a lot of things.

I was also sick, so I started to dream about my mother. She would be there, just as normal as I remember her. I would be stunned by her presence and just as she seemed to say something, I would wake up.

2

Of course, my life would have been different if my mother hadn't died when I was young. I know that I've made my choices, but losing her made me lose my way completely. My life is divided into *with my mother* and *without my mother*. She was, and still is, the only one who could make feel loved.

My mother had a liveliness about her that gave everything color. Plus, she was beautiful. She was a Kansas girl with a mix of Irish and Cherokee, but came to New York and tried to be a model. She wasn't so good in front of the camera, so she found her way behind it. No matter what she did, she had life.

Although many have tried to convince me otherwise, I know it was my fault that she died. The date was April 10th in New York, 14 years ago. I was in the 8th grade. Because she died, I remember it in every detail. Had she lived, it wouldn't have been a remarkable day at all. It was raining as we were stepping outside to get a taxi. Goldie was the doorman and adored my mother. The day wasn't a normal one anyway, as we usually took the train, but we were going by taxi to 'run some errands,' my mother said.

My memory of that morning haunts me. We were tense with each other and she was visibly upset. I was 13 and had gotten into trouble at school. They suspended me for something that I was a passive participant in, standing around while my friend smoked. For my mother, smoking was a horrible offense. Her own mother had been sick from it and caused mine to despise it. I'd gotten into a lot of trouble at school ever since my father ran off a few months earlier. It wasn't that we missed him much. He was unhappy with us. I received a full scholarship to the Upper West Side School due to sympathy.

On that day, we were supposed to go to a conference. She had to take a day off work. We were heading out early to do some errands, beforehand. I was worried that if I lost my scholarship there would be nothing to do because we were broke. Also, the smoking was the least of our offenses and I was scared that somehow Tom and I had been found out.

Goldie could tell that my mother wasn't herself and tried to cheer her with conversation. My mother was always friendly and social. Finally, a cab came and before we got in, Goldie said, "You have a blessed day."

3

I like to think I'm a fairly perceptive person, but I was preoccupied with the meeting. Tom hadn't been helpful when I'd snuck in a phone call to tell him what happened. The cab smelled so awful that I tried to open a window. My mother looked miserable and was carsick. I told the driver to stop and let us out. It wasn't a great place to get out, but my mother couldn't go any further. I gave the driver some money and we got out on upper 5th Avenue, by the park.

Once in the fresh air, she seemed to feel a bit better. When I asked why she didn't sit in the front seat, she said I sounded like my father. That returned the tension and I tried to appease her. I was starving, but didn't want to bother her, so we went to sit in the park. She said it was like a time warp and reminded her of when she was 18-years-old, getting off the bus from Kansas. As she was reminiscing, the rain returned and we rushed to somewhere dry. We ended up in the museum.

4

When my mother first arrived in New York, three major things happened to her. First, while working as a waitress, a booking agent offered her $1,000 to fill in as a catalogue model. With the money she earned modeling, she saved up and put herself through college as an Art History major at New York University. She hadn't seen great paintings until she came to New York, and then she was hooked. The third thing was meeting my father and having me. If she hadn't done the third, she would have gone further with her studies.

I liked the museum for its sheer size and I would often wander around until I got lost inside the maze of historical artifacts. My mother suggested that when we were finished she could complete one of the errands, buying a gift for someone at her advertising firm. She liked her job behind the camera and was good at it, though she worked a lot. She would have preferred to have gone back to school, but now that it was just the two of us, that wasn't going to happen.

Since we didn't have a lot of time, my mother quickly worked us through the exhibit. She was particularly interested in seeing the painting titled *The Anatomy Lesson* by Vermeer's teacher. As we wound through the rooms, she would stop and comment on a few pieces here and there. She would give some information about the artist or point out interesting features of the work.

There were a few other people in the museum and I took notice of a girl with bright red hair. I didn't know her, but I kept noticing her. When we came upon the painting my mother wanted to see, she was drawn in. She told me that it was the first painting she fell in love with as a kid in Kansas. She'd seen it in a library book.

At that time, the red-haired girl and an old man came up next to us. They were listening to my mother talk about the painting. I was a bit embarrassed by her excitement, but I was drawn to the girl and the old man. I wanted to know about her, but my mother was drawn into talking about the context of the painting and the artist. I was always more drawn to interesting-looking people. I would watch them on the streets and wonder about their lives. This girl and the old man were going to be on my mind for a while. I had so many questions about them.

As I started to daydream, my mother brought me back to reality and said we needed to make a move as the time was coming up for the school conference. She still wanted to look for a gift, but she couldn't help but go back to see *The Anatomy Lesson* just one more time. I said I would meet her at the gift shop and she walked away.

I was now free to speak to the girl with the old man, but when I had the courage, they were gone. I made my way towards the gift shop when I saw a guard run across the doorway, carrying something. Then, I saw the girl and the old man. Suddenly, there was a flash and a hot wind hit me, throwing me across the room. I blacked out.

5

I slowly returned to consciousness, completely confused as to where I was and what had happened. I felt as if someone had been beating me, but couldn't remember why. I was in a white cave with debris hanging from the ceiling. There were piles of rubble, garbage and all sorts of things on the ground. My ears were ringing and so was my body. It was a strange sensation.

I could hear something like alarms in the distance, but I couldn't get my bearings. I managed to stand myself up, but had a major pain in my head. My whole body hurt and I was cut up. I saw a shoe and a walking stick. I thought I heard a phone. I began to sift through the rubble to see if I could find the phone. I never could. I found a bottle of water and tried to understand what happened.

I saw movement. It was the old man. He was severely injured. He reached out with a surprisingly strong grip and tried to talk to me. He was in bad shape. I still didn't know where I was, but started to recall a video I'd seen on the Internet after a hotel was blown up. I stood back up to get the bottle of water as the man watched me with hope in his eyes. It was hot to the touch, but I drank half of it before taking it to the old man. He grabbed my face and tried to console me.

It was an odd, but unforgettable moment that passed between us. After trying to drink some water, he said, "Pippa". It started to think that I'd seen this man before and that I knew who Pippa was, but I wasn't sure how. He became agitated and I tried to calm him. He was confusing me with someone else. I tried to correct him, but he kept talking about music and auditions and events that I didn't know of but must have been from his past. He faded in and out, then tried to talk to me, realizing I wasn't who he thought I was. My head was pounding. Something about a striped umbrella entered my thoughts and I started to have a clearer view of the debris around me. It included body shapes and personal belongings.

The man started shaking me. He was pointing at a rectangle of board and said something about people stealing it or putting it in another place. I did as he asked and picked up the board. It was a painting I'd seen in the same book as *The Anatomy Lesson*. I was confused again. My thoughts came around to wondering where my mother was. I thought she was with me and the old man, but she wasn't there now. I took the picture to the man, but he said to take it with me. I needed to find my mother. The old man was recalling a past incident where his house was destroyed, and he wanted to save this painting.

I was confused and as the man stood up, I tried to tell him to sit back down. I tried to console him, but he kept reliving memories of packing his precious items and getting away from whatever attacked him. My head was hurting and I forgot my mother. I talked to the man and he returned to the present. He said he knew my mother, like he knew I'd been thinking of her.

I was having a hard time staying in the present, myself. The old man was giving me a ring and telling me to ring the green bell at Hobart and Blackwell. I had no idea what this meant. I took the ring and remembered what he said. He had a burst of energy and just as quickly lost it. I offered water, but he was gone.

Leaving him undisturbed, I began to scan the space, again. I could just make out a door that was blocked, so I turned the other direction, but that was blocked by fire. The door was covered, but I could move the debris. I put the painting in a bag and went through the door. It smelled terrible, and the dust was worse. I made my way through in the dark, climbing over things. I tried to get at a flashlight in the bag, but instead turned a cellphone on. The light revealed a hand coming out the rubble. I eventually crawled out onto the floor of a gallery.

There was rescue equipment with FDNY on it, but there didn't appear to be anyone around. I called out, but there was no answer. Once I got to the open space, I could see that things weren't as they should be. The people were lying down. Some weren't in one piece. I didn't want to, but I forced myself to look at all the people. It was a relief that none of them were my mother. There was more equipment and blood, but the next area was empty, even of bodies. I found the gallery where she'd gone. There was nothing and no one but the faces of the paintings.

Suddenly, I was running. I ran and ran. There was no one around to direct me on how to get out, but I found familiar areas. I couldn't find my way out until I finally saw a door, barely visible in the wall. I walked through an office hallway, past people's desks and nameplates. I couldn't see well, but kept going, calling out, "Hello?" The office was never-ending, but I finally saw a door marked EXIT. I ran towards it and down the stairwell, and then I was outside in the rain. The sounds were deafening, but no one was there, waiting for me.

I'd come out in Central Park. I made my way back to the front of the museum, where vans were everywhere for the NYPD, FDNY, and other rescue units. Crime scene tape was up, but nobody was doing anything. I yelled, "You need to go back inside. People are still in there!" The attendant explained that there was another bomb and they had to evacuate. He never looked at me and before I could say more, a huge cop came and moved me to the other side of the street. He scared me. I hurried to another area, hoping to see my mother, but I didn't. There were ambulances waiting to take people.

It was a chaotic scene. As I tried to find my mother, the crowd became too much. I gave up and went with our agreed upon back up plan in emergencies, to meet at home. My head was throbbing and I tried to keep an eye out for her as I made my way towards home. I knew that she'd gotten out, because none of the bodies I'd seen were her. I was only concerned about whey she would have left without finding me.

Chapter Two: For the Love of a Painting

One of my greatest fears when I was young was that my mother wouldn't come home from work. I learned to add and subtract, quickly to help me keep tabs on when to expect her. If she were late, I would worry and if she were more than ten minutes late, I'd sit by the door, hoping to hear the elevator bringing her home. Every day on the news, I'd hear about some attack or crime and would worry that it might happen to her. My dad was still around in those days, but he was unreliable, so it worried me more to lose my mom.

I never understood why my dad was so unhappy with us. He blamed us for the job he hated, and he disliked everything we did. He would ignore me in the mornings and was hardly around in the evenings. When he got his paycheck, every other week, he would go out drinking and come back making a lot noise in the early hours. On those days, my mother and I would be careful not to do anything to disturb him or would work out a way to get out of the apartment. It didn't bother us too much when one day he just never came back. On the second day we started to worry a little and on the third day, his secretary called to say he hadn't shown up for work. My mother called the police and we waited.

At the end of the week, we got a note from Newark, New Jersey. He was going to start a new life somewhere. I didn't understand what that meant and had a hard time with it. Still, overall, it wasn't necessarily a bad thing that my father was gone. I hardly knew him, but it was difficult on my mother. She didn't make much money and without any support from my dad, we had to be careful.

The walk home from the museum is vague in my memory. My head was killing me and the rain was still coming down so I could hardly see. I heard various words like "North Korea" or "Iran" and "al-Qaeda" from people and radios, but nothing mattered. I just wanted to get home.

The phone lines were probably down, so I couldn't call even if I'd had my cell phone. I sent her messages in my mind, letting her know that I was okay and would see her soon. I thought of Pippa. She was the girl who kept me from going with my mother and maybe saved my life. I hoped someone had saved the old man. When I arrived at the apartment building, no one was around. Usually, a doorman was present, but it was empty. I took the elevator and felt relief to be finally home.

When I opened the door, it was still and quiet. I couldn't believe my mother wasn't home yet. I walked around trying to find some signs that she had been there, but everything was the same as we had left it in the morning. I thought I would look for messages on my phone, but I couldn't find it after she had taken it when I got suspended. So, I sat on the carpet trying to clear my head. There was a roaring sound in my ears and my head was on fire.

Finally, I must have lain down on the living room sofa. I came to upon hearing the sounds of doors and hoping that it meant my mother was home. It wasn't her. There was a message light blinking on the machine and with great hope I played it, expecting to hear my mother's voice. Instead, it was just a colleague, checking in with my mother. I couldn't believe it. Where could she be? I called her phone and left her messages, hoping she would get them. I tried to think of reasons why she wouldn't have her phone on or get back to me.

I walked around trying to find signs of her having been home, but nothing had changed. I wanted to go look for her, but what if she came back while I was out? Finally, I called down to the doorman, but none of the usual guys were there. I turned on the TV to see the news and understood why none of the doormen were there. The bridges were closed.

There was a number to call if anyone was missing. I decided to give her a half hour and then I would call. After waiting for an hour, I finally gave in and called the number. The woman said that my mother's name wasn't on the list, took my name and said they would call back if her name turned up. After I hung up, I realized that I didn't know what the list was for. I walked around trying to sort it out, but couldn't and finally called to ask what that meant.

"She's not listed among the dead or the injured," said the woman.

I felt positive then. She must be okay. The woman said it just meant that they didn't have any information. The woman again confirmed that they would call back if anything changed. I kept watching the news. Twenty-one people were dead and more were injured.

Despite my desire to go out and look for her, I stuck with our Family Disaster Plan, which was to meet at home. As I watched the TV, the death toll rose. I phoned again. They still didn't have anything. I tried to see if perhaps she was at a hospital or somewhere I could go to see her. They didn't have any information. The woman suggested I go down to the Armory where they had set up support for families, but I didn't want that information. She then asked me how old I was and I quickly hung up after that.

I was in shock and decided to try eating some of the leftover Chinese food from the previous night. There was more, but I left some for my mother in case she came home and was hungry. It seemed that finally some right wing extremists group had taken responsibility for the bombings at the museum. My head was still hurting, my ears were ringing and I tasted a tinny flavor in my mouth. Still, I tried to keep myself busy.

I kept myself glued to the television in hopes of hearing something that would tell me where my mother was. They interviewed the curator who was worried about the integrity of the artwork as well as the victims. Suddenly, the phone rang. I was so relieved that it had to be my mother, but then the caller ID showed NYDoCFS. I didn't know who that was.

I hesitantly picked up the phone, "Hello?"

A woman's voice answered, explaining that she was from the Department of Child and Family Services.

I asked if she was calling about my mother, but she wouldn't answer me. She kept asking me for my father, but I told her he couldn't come to the phone. She said she needed to speak to him and wouldn't give me any information. In the end, she left a phone number and left me with nothing. I sat very still after that, noticing the late time and the lack of life without my mother there. I could hear the traffic in the distance and knew that soon the city would start to come to life.

Then, what was I supposed to do? I tried to clear my head, but I was so tired and everything started to have a glow around it. I didn't want to call the police, so I was just about ready to go back out and look for her myself, despite the time. Just as I had made up my mind, the doorbell rang. I thought for sure it must be my mother, "Mom?"

My heart dropped when I opened the door to two people I didn't know. From the moment I saw them, I knew my life was about to change forever.

Chapter Three: The Barbours

1

The social workers at my door took me to a diner where they began to ask me questions. They also tried to get me to eat breakfast, but I don't remember anything except the smell of the eggs that left my stomach in knots. Due to the early hour, the diner was pretty empty. The social workers, Enrique and a Korean lady whose name I cannot recall, tried to get me to accept what they were saying. My mother had died. She had been hit in the head by debris and died instantly. Her body was at New York Hospital. Did I understand?

I understood the words they were saying, but I couldn't quite grasp what it meant for me. They moved on to ask me about my father and when I had last seen him. I didn't know how to answer that. I guessed it had been shortly after the school year began. My head was still killing me whenever I moved. They were not satisfied with my lack of knowledge and kept asking me for information I didn't know or have.

Finally, after the plates were taken away, it became clearer as to why they were asking me about my father and then my grandparents. I was a minor without a guardian. They needed to get in touch with my family. Until then, I was under the protection of the city. What did that mean exactly? Enrique explained to me that I was going to be placed into emergency custody in the city. That freaked me out. I knew about the temporary homes and I wasn't going to go there. I asked what would happen if I didn't want to go. They said that if I could find somebody to stay with until they reached my family, it would be a possible solution.

For some reason, an old friend from elementary school, Andy Barbour popped into my head. I quickly gave them his name and phone number. I had basically known them my whole life and Andy had been my best friend at one time. Andy's dad worked on Wall Street, but had some mental issues and his mother was a socialite stay-at-home kind of mom. Enrique and the Korean lady promised to check it out and said they were willing to take me there if the Barbours were okay with it. Enrique went outside and was on the phone while we waited inside.

We made a stop at the apartment for me to get a few things and then went to Park Avenue in the upper Sixties, where the Barbours lived. I remembered the doormen, though I hadn't been there in a while. The doorman who greeted us gave me the first of many sympathy looks and told us to go up.

2

Mr. Barbour opened the door and let us all in. Inside, Mrs. Barbour greeted us as she was pouring coffee.

The social workers perused the apartment that was immaculately decorated and showed the fact that she came from money. She also knew just how to carry herself and immediately took charge of the situation once we were in her domain.

Mrs. Barbour turned her attention to me and explained where I would be staying, offering me some food and then asking what they could do for me. Since I had no idea, Mr. Barbour made the move to get me settled in. He took me to Andy's brother's room, who was away at school and tried to comfort me but there was nothing anyone could do for me. Not knowing quite what to do, he left me alone and shortly after that, Mrs. Barbour brought Andy in, whom they had woken from his sleep. Andy said a few words and then we sat in silence.

3

It was a horrible time to go through. People were overly nice and there was always food being offered. People would come to see me, like the social worker, a city appointed psychiatrist and some of my mother's friends. They all had little stories and memories to share with me about her. Mrs. Barbour did her best to protect me and kept most visits short in her polite, but commanding way.

Life continued as normal in the Barbour house with the maids, nannies, caterers, tutors and so on coming and going. Andy had a younger brother and sister who played around in the halls as if all was normal. They never seemed to let on if they were inconvenienced by the extra presence of me in the house. Mrs. Barbour always looked out for me when it came to the press, Enrique's grillings about where my father might be and so on. She went so far as to remove any newspapers or other chance of me hearing anything about the bombing or my mother's death.

Luckily, Andy and I got along as great as we had before. We had bonded in elementary school when we had both been pushed up a grade and then bullied for different reasons. Somehow we had grown apart once we hit junior high. Andy went the super nerd way and I didn't. Still, in the first days, Andy stayed home from school to hang out with me. In between keeping up with his schoolwork, we would play chess or watch TV together.

When Andy studied, I would count how many days had passed since that day. I would recall what we had eaten on those days or other things I could remember. At night, I would really miss my mother. I felt like dying because I missed her so much. I tried to hold on to all of the best memories with her. I would think of all the ways her death could have been prevented. For example, I could have insisted that I wanted to eat breakfast. The day of the conference at school could have been changed.

A few nights after my mother's death, I was finally taken to the doctor to treat my headache. Things were okay but I kept having the feeling that I was lost and disoriented. I wanted to go home.

4

Eventually, Andy had to go back to school and I spent the days watching movies on Turner Classic Movies because that was what my mother liked to watch. A couple more days later, Mrs. Barbour announced that I was going to go back to school the next day. There was nothing I could say, so I let Mrs. Barbour convince me that returning to 'normal' was good for me. I didn't want to go back to school. Going back would mean the acceptance that my mother had died and I was still holding onto that denial.

I managed to get myself to school though I knew it would be horrible. It was. Everything kept moving and going even though my world had ended. People said they were sorry to me, even people I'd never talked to before. Other people went silent when I went by, but never said anything. Still others ignored me as if acknowledging me would acknowledge my tragedy.

Tom Cable was the strangest of all. He was the one I'd gotten caught with for smoking. He and I had spent summers getting into trouble together. We always had this 'too cool for life' attitude with one another, but he was really weird with me. At first, he talked to me brusquely as if I hadn't just had a major traumatic event happen to me. Eventually, he completely stopped talking to me.

I wasn't hurt or depressed about his behavior towards me. I was angry. If it hadn't been for him, I wouldn't have gotten suspended and my mother and I wouldn't have been on our way to a conference at school. She would still be alive.

I didn't expect him to take responsibility, but he was treating me like I had done something to him. I wanted to hurt him, but found that other people who had never

talked to me before were suddenly kind to me. The adults
were really the worst though. They were telling me
different ways to cope, giving me advice to deal with my
grief or giving me compliments a lot. Perhaps I was coping
quite well with everything, but I would get these waves of
sadness and feel as if the whole world had been destroyed.
For me it had.

5

My father's parents never crossed my mind. When
the social workers finally found them and said that my
grandmother was in poor health and couldn't take me, it
wasn't a real disappointment. They offered to let me stay in
a nearby hotel, which they would pay for. I felt ashamed
because even though I hadn't really wanted to stay with my
grandparents, now I knew that they didn't want me either. I
was told I would stay with the Barbours a bit longer, even
through the end of the school year.

Mrs. Barbour noticed that I was playing with the
ring which the old man had given me in the museum after
the explosion. She asked me a lot of questions and looked
carefully at it. I had taken to carrying it around everywhere

and sometimes wearing it on my finger even though it was much too big. Mrs. Barbour admired it as an old relic and asked if Blackwell meant anything. I recalled then that the old man had told me that name. I had difficulty remembering everything from the event at the time.

As Mrs. Barbour continued to examine the ring, I asked her what would happen to me if my grandparents didn't want me. For a brief moment, she didn't know what to say, but quickly recovered and told me not to worry about it for now. She left me alone and cautioned me against losing the ring. She said that I should put it somewhere safe.

6

Of course, I didn't take Mrs. Barbour's advice on the ring. I kept wearing and carrying it around with me. It somehow made me feel stable, even though I didn't want to recall how I got it. Thinking about the future was almost as bad. Even though everyone else seemed upset by the offer to stay at a Holiday Inn, it was becoming more appealing as I really had nowhere else to go. Besides, being on my own in a hotel would be pretty nice.

All the adults around me kept saying it wasn't possible, but I didn't clearly understand why. Dave, my city psychiatrist kept trying to convince me not to worry and that I would be taken care of. When I kept going back to the idea of living in a hotel, he broke it down for me. I was only 13 years old. I was a minor. I couldn't live alone.

He was hopeful that something would be worked out with my grandparents, but he didn't know them. I had my doubts since the last time I'd seen them was probably five years before and there wasn't a great connection between us. My mother had wanted me to know my father's family, but after the last visit we never went back.

Some days after my grandparents had said they couldn't take me, we received a letter from them expressing their condolences and apologies for not being able to take care of me. Andy tried to console me, but it didn't make any sense. He suggested to his parents that I could continue to stay with them. They politely agreed, but said that they shouldn't keep me from my family. What family?

7

It was very difficult to blend into the world of the Barbours, even though I tried extra hard to be good. Luckily, Mr. and Mrs. Barbour weren't around much, so I couldn't be in their way much. They were busy with social events or work. The hardest part was dealing with Andy's little brother and sister. His older brother, Platt was gone away for school. Still, it was clear that I got more attention from the adult Barbours than their own kids did. I could tell this caused a bit of jealousy amongst them.

8

I had to return to our apartment before the movers came and put our belongings in storage. I recalled that I had taken a painting on that fateful day and knew that I should have probably told someone about it. I had had opportunities, like when investigators came to talk to me, but Mrs. Barbour had shooed them away. Three days later, the investigators returned, but came for me at school. I was taken out of my geometry class to the principal's conference room and saw everyone who had anything to do with me in the room.

The investigators tried to appease me by saying that they just wanted to put some pieces of the puzzle together with my help and that I didn't have to worry. I was scared. I still hadn't grasped the fact that I was a minor and so a guardian had to be present for these interviews. It was just that I had a lot of guardians at the time.

The investigators began with some easy questions, but they weren't putting me at ease. They changed tactics, telling me they just wanted to know what I remembered from that day. For example, they started with what I ate for breakfast. I gave them a totally made up answer. Everyone knew it and the principal, Mr. Beeman interjected that I didn't need to make up answers if I didn't have them. The school counselor, Mrs. Swanson explained that I had some memory loss because I had hit my head.

There was some tension around the room when the investigators asked if I'd been taken to a doctor, because I had gone so much later than I should have. In any case, the investigators got back to business. They wanted me to describe everything in detail and kept asking the same questions in different ways. I thought they were going to ask me about the painting and that stressed me out.

They showed me floor maps of the museum, trying to determine where I was, but none of it made sense to me. I kept saying, "I don't know," but they kept pushing me. I felt near tears when Mr. Beeman finally interjected about the necessity of all these questions. The investigators seemed peeved that their job was being questioned. There was another tense moment that passed and the investigators continued. Mr. Beeman was not appeased and interrupted again. The investigators asked if he was obstructing the proceedings. Mr. Beeman finally stopped.

They continued to ask me about the map and what I remembered. When I couldn't come up with anything, it was suddenly over. Mrs. Barbour took the investigator's card on my behalf, should I recall anything further later on. When people were getting ready to leave, Mrs. Swanson and Dave seemed prepared to ensure that I was alright, but what I wanted was to return to a normal day.

9

The questioning disoriented me and suddenly things I thought I had forgotten came back to me, like the smells, lights and so on. This always happened when I didn't expect it. There hadn't been any photographs for the old man and the red-haired girl. I felt the ring again in my pocket and felt a connection with the two. It was a blood connection, having shared the accident together.

10

Mrs. Barbour had started giving me Elavil, which was a green pill to help me sleep. It seemed that I was having nightmares or dreams of my mother being alive, and waking up Andy a lot. With the pill I went into a deep sleep. Mr. Barbour suggested black tea to help me wake up out of my stupor. I hadn't been hungry much since the accident and I could tell that Mrs. Barbour was concerned. She kept offering me different foods, but I didn't want anything. This caused the jealousy of the younger siblings to rise, but their parents promptly ignored it.

11

It was a Sunday morning when I was coming out of a dream stupor and clearly remembered something from my last moments with the old man: *Hobart and Blackwell. Ring the green bell*. I was not yet sure about the reality of the dream as I'd had difficulty separating the two in the past. When I finally woke up, I looked for Andy, but he was already up.

Sunday breakfasts were a big deal for the Barbours. They were already at the table, so I took the opportunity to stop in the family room and see if I could find Hobart and Blackwell in the White Pages. Surprisingly, I found them with an address and telephone number. I dialed the number, but as I was waiting for someone to answer, Mrs. Barbour had stealthily arrived and asked what I was doing. I said, "Nothing," and she said that breakfast was waiting.

When I joined, Platt was in my usual spot since he was home to attend a party the night before. Mr. Barbour reintroduced me to Platt as he went to get another chair for me. Mr. Barbour was again trying to convince the family that sailing was something worth loving, aside from the fact that it was also a birthright. Andy was arguing against it since he really hated it. It seemed that no one in the family was really keen on it other than Mr. Barbour.

I was distracted by the lack of answer to my phone call and when I could get away without eating I went back to the family room. Andy snuck up behind me, asking whom I was calling. I knew I could trust him, so I explained about the old man and the girl and the connection I felt to them. Andy asked if they were in the city and I gave him the address. He told me that if they weren't answering the phone, I should just go down there in person.

I was hesitant to do that, but Andy gave a good argument. He offered to go with me but I knew he had his usual studying and school activities to do that day, so I thanked him anyway. He gave me his cell phone just in case I needed it, though I didn't think I did.

12

Just around midday, I was on the bus heading to the Village with the Hobart and Blackwell address written down. It's not easy to find addresses in the Village, but eventually I did. The place looked old and deserted. It was some kind of antique store, but most didn't open until noon on Sundays, so I walked around to pass the time. I tried to walk around and even stepped into a place my mother and I would eat at. I felt uncomfortable. I went back to Hobart and Blackwell. It didn't look like it was going to open or even that it had been opened in some time. I didn't know what to do next.

As I was looking in the window, I saw a shape go near the back of the shop. Then, I recalled that I should ring the green bell. I looked around, but didn't see one. After some searching, I finally saw it down a narrow door well.

I rang the bell and to my surprise, a very tall man answered the door. He wasn't dressed well, but was impressive enough that I forgot why I was there for a moment. Finally, I found my voice and started to explain, but couldn't, and just held out the ring to him. He had just been watching me, but upon seeing the ring, he asked where I had gotten it. I explained that the old man had given it to me and said to bring it here. He stared at me for a moment and finally, opened the door for me to pass through. He introduced himself as Hobie.

Chapter Four: Pippa

1

I followed the tall man through the workshop and into a room that kept out the sun. It looked like death had visited here. I suddenly regretted having come, but the man seemed to notice my discomfort and looked concerned. We both were at a loss for words. He was a middle-aged man with neither handsome nor ugly features. He was big, but graceful at the same time.

I offered to come back another time, but he said no. He was as shocked as I was to be in this situation. The place was a bit of a mess and he cleared a place for me to sit. To ease the tension, I quickly introduced myself to which he did the same. He was James Hobart, called Hobie. Welty, the old man, was his business partner and had died in the explosion. The investigators told Hobie the same thing they told me about my mother. He died instantly. My presence and story showed that not to be true. Hobie said he was glad that Welty wasn't alone at the end.

It was awkward again. Hobie mentioned how Welty's body had been hard to look at and related it to seeing Mathew Brady's photos of the Civil War. For some reason, I blurted out all the knowledge that I had about the war. Hobie asked me for more details about the last moments of Welty's life. I answered the best that I could. I also realized that perhaps my mother had lived longer than I was told since they had given me the same story.

I asked about the girl. Hobie hesitated, so I asked if she was alright. He explained that she was alive, but it wasn't clear yet how she was. It turned out that she was there, but he wasn't sure if I should see her or not.

He recognized me as the boy whose mother had died, but when I was shocked by the recognition, he got flustered and changed the subject. He offered me food, but that annoyed me since it seemed that adults always wanted to feed me. He asked me to humor him and took me into the kitchen. As I followed him, I saw pictures and recognized Mr. Blackwell and young Pippa.

I asked if that was her, but Hobie said it was her mother, Juliet. Juliet had died of cancer six years before. Welty was her big half brother, but due to their age difference of thirty years, he'd practically raised her as his own. We continued down the hall and I saw a door, but Hobie quietly closed it, saying I couldn't see her yet.

In the kitchen, Hobie explained that the girl had had a skull fracture that required five surgeries to fix and she was still in a fragile state. I asked if she was going to be okay. He said they didn't know, that they hoped so, but she was in a lot of pain and couldn't stay up very long.

I asked Hobie if he knew how she had gotten out. He told me that she had luckily been rescued at the beginning, before they were told to evacuate. I must have still been out of it, because I didn't recall any of that.

Hobie set some food in front of me, toast and cheese, as he prepared some tea. I took a bite and found that I really liked it. It was the first time that I had eaten in what was probably forever. While I ate, Hobie asked me different questions, normal questions about what I liked and about school. Most adults didn't talk to me like that. We began to talk about just about anything and everything. I even talked about my father.

Hobie knew of Mrs. Barbour as she was from a very good family and was very active in the city. Welty had known her more. I wondered how he knew that I was staying with them. He told me it was in the newspaper. That was what had been kept from me at the Barbours. It was the first time I was hearing about this. Apparently, the news article had been very flattering towards me describing how I had protected Andy. I was embarrassed as it wasn't a big deal to me.

I asked if Hobie was going to open the shop again or not. He didn't seem sure since Welty had been the one to take care of the business. Hobie worked in the workshop doing repairs to antiques and such. Our conversation was interrupted by Andy texting me from a friend's phone, checking to make sure I was okay. I didn't respond. Hobie and I sat quietly together. I thanked him for the food. He asked me about a piece that I had noticed in the hallway, Noah's ark. I asked if it was hers, but he said no. It was one of the first antiques he'd bought. I asked again if I could see her. He finally agreed and warned me that her mind was confused about events from the explosion.

2

The room was also dark, but I could see the outline of objects. Hobie told her I was there to see her and she stirred. "Hi," she said to me, "Who are you?"

I introduced myself. She asked me my favorite piece of music. I had no idea and just said Beethoven. She remembered me, but not the details of why she knew me. I lied to her, saying we were friends when she asked. We had a bit more conversation about music and she asked me if I got tired during the day. After my mother died, I had started falling asleep in school and in the afternoons.

When Hobie stepped out of the room, I took her hand. It was the first time for me to do something like that and she asked if she could close her eyes a bit. I could see she was tired again. I left her and returned to Hobie. The nurse came and I took that as my cue to leave. I asked if I could come back and he said, of course I could. In fact, he seemed eager for me to return.

3

When I got back to the Barbours, Andy wanted the details as we were getting ready for dinner. I told him that Hobie knew his mom and that it was a little weird, but I was really glad that I went. I gave him back his phone.

Andy suddenly and unexpectedly apologized for my situation. He'd really liked my mom. He said he missed her and that it must be even worse for me. I didn't know how to respond. He kept talking about memories of her. It bothered me a bit, but I knew he meant well.

4

Over the next week, my appetite returned and everyone took note of it. The younger siblings made a big deal of it, saying I had ended my hunger strike.

5

My next psychiatric session involved Dave trying to get me to reveal why I had seemingly changed. I didn't feel like talking to him. He asked me about my meds, but the truth was that I had stopped taking them by spitting them down the drain in the sink. He managed to get me to admit that I was feeling better. I wasn't really better, though. I was more emotional. Sometimes I was happy and other times I just wanted to cry. Dave tried to reassure me of his role and that he just wanted to let me talk. If I didn't want to talk, he was okay with that too. He asked me to help him understand the change, but I couldn't explain.

6

Several days later, I asked if Andy would cover for me so I could go back to the Village. He willingly agreed and came up with an excuse to give his mother.

7

Hobie answered the door quickly. He was looking cleaner than the first time I saw him. I asked if it was a bad time and he assured me it was fine. He'd been hoping that I would come by. Something wasn't quite right though and I asked him about it, noticing that the dog that usually stayed in Pippa's room was in the kitchen.

Pippa's Aunt Margaret from Texas was there to take Pippa back with her. Margaret was the other half-sister of Welty, though they hadn't been close. She was the closest relative and had the right to make decisions. I asked how Pippa was doing. Hobie said she was doing much better and had even asked about me. She'd said I would come back just the day before and there I was.

The decision for her to move was pretty final. There had been a lot of preparations going on for the move. Hobie tried to be positive about it, but I could see that he was actually sad. A young grandmother type of woman came out and asked what was going on. Hobie explained who I was and suddenly she was charming. I asked if I could see Pippa and Hobie replied that I could.

8

The light was on and when I entered the room, Pippa asked if I could turn it off. I could see that things had been cleared out. She was listening to something on her iPod and shared her ear buds with me. It was a small connection between us. She told me about her leaving. She didn't want to go. Margaret had told her about the horses that were in Texas and we started talking about how my mother had liked them. She said again that she didn't want to go, but everyone had decided it was best for her.

I said that I might have to go live with my grandparents and I didn't want to go either. We talked some more and I told her that I didn't want her to go. She kissed me. I asked her if she remembered seeing me just before the accident. She didn't. Then, Hobie was at the door. They talked a bit and then it was time for me to say goodbye. We promised to write and Margaret suggested that I come to Texas sometime to visit. I wasn't paying attention, remembering the sweet flavor of her kiss and reveling in the visit all the way back to the Barbours.

9

On the day that Pippa was supposed to leave, Andy tried to cheer me up, saying Texas wasn't that interesting, but that it would probably be better for her in the end. He reasoned that the climate was better.

10

Though the Barbour house was always busy and full, I felt very lonely. The end of the school year was approaching and I still had no idea as to what was going to happen to me. The Barbours were planning on going to their summerhouse in Maine, but nothing had been said about me. Andy wasn't very excited about going, and tried to make it sound more interesting for me if I were to end up with my grandparents instead.

I wasn't as convinced. Andy suggested a particular outlook, should I be forced to move to Maryland. He recommended that I do my very best in school and get a scholarship to go to any college that I wanted. I explained that my grades weren't that great, but he was convinced that any public school that I would end up at would be easy. Since I'd been moved up, like him, due to high testing, it would be easy for me to get good grades.

Andy reassured me that I was smart. He mentioned that adults liked me because I was polite and did what I was supposed to do. I asked him if he had it all figured out, then why hadn't he sorted out his sailing problem with his father. It seemed that Andy had already thought this through. He had just four more summers to survive until he could hopefully go to college early and would never have to get on another boat again.

11

I was visiting Hobie again and he talked about how hard it was for him to talk to Pippa on the phone. Apparently, she wasn't adjusting very well and had cried for three hours after their last conversation. Margaret was working to get Pippa settled and had hired a therapist who used the horses to help with rehabilitation. Hobie knew how hard that must be for Pippa since she had spent most of her life in the world of music in New York City.

I asked why Pippa hadn't known Margaret before. Hobie explained the complicated situation of Welty's father having three children with three different women. According to Margaret, she and her father were close, but when Pippa's mother came along, Margaret felt betrayed and wanted nothing to do with Juliet or her family.

She had been away in college at the time. Later, their father had gotten tired of Juliet's mother and decided to leave that entire part of the family out of his will. Welty had felt bad for how things turned out and took on Juliet as his own. After telling more of the story of Welty, Hobie showed me the workshop where he did all his work in refurbishing antique furniture. I enjoyed looking at all the things in his workshop. Hobie asked if I liked old things. I did. It was the first time I realized it, but I did.

Hobie thought that since I liked old stuff I should like the Barbours' place, but it was different in the workshops. He asked me how so. I explained that when all the types of furniture were put together I could see the different 'personalities' of the various styles, but when they were separated it was hard to understand or appreciate the value of the pieces. Hobie claimed that I had a good idea for furniture and asked if I had time to help him out with a piece he was working on.

12

The adults wanted me to have a hobby, but I wasn't interested in the things they were suggesting. Mrs. Swanson said the main point was to find a way for me to connect with other people. It was part of the plan to help me get over the death of my mother. I resented the intent.

I was fighting their push for a hobby, but I had developed one by helping Hobie in his workshop two or three times a week. I was learning a great deal from him and enjoying it. Even more than the new hobby, I enjoyed spending time with Hobie. We had in depth talks about anything and everything. He always treated me like an equal, which no other adult ever did. He shared a lot of stories about himself, which I found comforting.

My regular absences were becoming more difficult to hide from Mrs. Barbour. Hobie offered to speak with her directly or invite her down to the store, as she might like some of the pieces. I wasn't sure what would be the best action to take. I said I would think about it. As I was thinking on my way home, Mrs. Barbour met me at the door, wanting to know where I had been. It seemed that Andy's excuses weren't working anymore.

I decided to tell her a version of the truth. I said I had been going to visit a friend of my mother's downtown. That seemed to appease Mrs. Barbour. I mentioned that she might know him, which piqued her interest. She didn't seem convinced that it was a real person, so when she asked if she could call him, I quickly agreed and even told her that he had suggested we all get together. She wasn't expecting that response, but seemed happy with it. She apologized for not trusting me. I asked Andy what was wrong. Something had happened with Platt at school that had upset her. He didn't know exactly what, but it must have been bad if he was sent home.

13

After the confrontation and problems at home with Platt, I stayed around for Andy's sake and didn't visit Hobie for a few days. He claimed that his parents were better when I was around. We kept trying to figure out what it was that Platt had done, but we couldn't guess.

14

The idea of telling someone about the painting came up again. It was still in the apartment where I had left it. I had kept quiet for so long that I wasn't sure how to go about bringing it up. The more I worked with Hobie, the worse I felt for not telling someone.

It's not that I wanted to keep it. If I could have given it back anonymously, I absolutely would have, but I couldn't find a way to do it that way. There were only two people I would consider telling, Hobie or Mrs. Barbour, but it still seemed somewhat crazy to just decide to tell someone now after all this time. As I was contemplating what to do, I saw a newspaper article about the painting. The museum declared the painting - *The Goldfinch*, a 1654 masterpiece by Carel Fabritius - as lost in the explosion.

As I was reading the details, Mrs. Barbour came in to propose that I join them in Maine for the summer. I was surprised and happy at the same time. I quickly and emphatically agreed. She seemed pleased. She explained that Mr. Barbour and the kids would leave first. She would follow after finishing up a few things in the city. Andy seemed happy as well, though he warned me that sailing wasn't going to be as exciting as I might think.

15

The good news about the painting being declared as destroyed and being invited to join the Barbours for the summer gave me such relief. I began to think that perhaps the summer invitation meant a more long-term decision about my status in the family. I knew I should do something about the painting, but became too consumed with thoughts about the summer until all thoughts about the painting were lost.

16

Hobie was telling me about his father. He thought that Hobie was too educated, so all payments for his college were stopped. In exchange for college tuition, Hobie was to work at his father's trucking company. His father hadn't kept his side of the bargain. I was shocked to hear this. Hobie said that he then realized he would grow old without ever getting out of his situation and didn't know how he could escape. That was when Welty entered his life. He'd been a client of his father's for a while and they both liked him. Welty had been around one day when Hobie's father was laying in on him and telephoned his father the next day asking if Hobie could help him pack up some furniture.

That was his door to freedom from his father. Welty paid him in cash that day and offered him work in the shop in New York. He never looked back even though his father refused to talk to him ever again. Hobie had learned his trade the same way that I was learning. The man who used to work there before him taught him everything via observation. He had never gone back to college because he found what he liked to do.

His point in telling me this story was that I never knew what kind of opportunities were going to present themselves over the summer. I may find that I love sailing. More than finding what I liked to do, I had a secret hope that a decision would be made about me in the Barbour family. Andy thought they were going to keep me for good and would make the announcement in Maine.

17

When I arrived back home at the Barbours that day, something was wrong. Mrs. Barbour asked me to join them in Mr. Barbour's study. When I went into the room, a man greeted me. It was my father. He had changed since I'd last seen him but I wasn't happy to see him. The Barbours shared my feeling, but there was nothing they could do. He was my father. With my father was a woman who introduced herself as Xandra, with an X, and not pronounced like Sandra. I was shocked and confused.

They had just arrived in the city and had come straight to the Barbours. My father explained that he was in Las Vegas now. They had come to get me. Xandra made a point of letting me know that my father had been sober for 51 days. She claimed that it was because she couldn't handle him drunk anymore. It dawned on me that this was probably the person he had left me and my mother for. She was his 'fresh start'.

My father wasted no time and told me that they had come straight from the airport because they needed to get into our apartment. They had already tried to get in, but the locks had been changed when he left us. I remembered some fights where my mother knew that my father had taken some of her jewelry even though he got angry and denied it. When he left, some things went missing to prove that my mother wasn't wrong. She changed the locks.

There was no knowing what to do or say to him. I just stood there. Finally, he asked if I could do something to help them out. I lied and said I didn't have a key. My father suggested getting a locksmith. I didn't want them there alone since the painting was there, so I quickly suggested that the doormen would let us in if I were there.

18

We arrived at the building and I greeted Jose. He recognized me right away and greeted me kindly. He also politely greeted my father and Xandra. Before my father could say anything, I used the some of the Spanish I had learned to ask Jose to open the apartment and if he would come in with us. My father couldn't understand, so Jose understood what I was doing. He politely agreed in English and carried on a casual conversation with Xandra as we made our way to the apartment.

Once Jose opened the door, I could immediately smell the staleness in the apartment. I went quickly to get the bag with the painting in it hoping to get it out before my father noticed. When I picked up the bag, it wasn't as heavy as it should have been. I panicked before realizing that I'd left it on the bureau in my mother's bedroom so she would see it when she came home.

Xandra was still chatting away with Jose, so I made my way to my mother's bedroom. I grabbed the painting and went into my room across the hall. Just as I was trying to figure out how to get it covered up with my musty clothes, my father appeared, asking what I was doing.

He suspiciously asked about the bag I left in the hall and I said it was my school bag even though it was atypical for such a bag. He took a whiff of it and said that it stunk. While he was distracted, I managed to cover the painting mostly. My father noticed something and asked what it was. I explained it was just a poster. He suddenly tried to explain that my mother hadn't been easy for him to live with. He couldn't keep up with her moods and told me that there were always two sides to every story. His was quite different from hers. Though they had both been unhappy, he hadn't wished for her to die.

Still, he harbored some resentment. I'd never heard or seen his point of view before. I wasn't really interested in hearing his side of things and just wanted to get the painting somewhere safe. Xandra appeared, complimenting the place and then my father took her to my mother's bedroom. I didn't like the idea of them going through her things but I quickly got out a suitcase and wrapped the painting in a newspaper. I packed some clothes into it, put in the painting and packed more clothes on top.

While my father and Xandra were violating my mother's things, I went to the lobby to talk to Jose. As I was going out to get him, a voice stopped me. It was Goldie. I hadn't seen him since that day. It was awkward. He talked about that day and how he felt when he heard the news. As he talked, Jose came inside. They began talking about how great my mother was and how different from most people.

Jose noticed my suitcase and asked if I needed a cab. Instead, I asked him to keep it in the backroom for me. I insisted that they give it to no one but me. Jose didn't ask any questions and immediately put it on the top shelf in the room where only the doormen used the space. Jose understood because some guys had come around looking for my dad. Jose told them we didn't live there anymore and they hadn't come back. As we were talking, Goldie came in with a load of cash and handed it to me. He explained that my mom had paid for a computer that was delivered and he hadn't been able to afford though his son needed it for school. He was paying her back now. I wasn't sure I bought his story, but I took it and put it in my pocket before my dad and Xandra showed up and before anyone from the streets saw it.

19

That night, my dad and Xandra took me out to
dinner. My dad was calling the insurance company about
my mother's death. Xandra regaled me with stories about
herself. After my father finished his phone call, he ordered
a bottle of champagne. He had quit drinking, but she
hadn't. She couldn't drink the whole bottle herself and
suggested I help her. She filled up my glass.

Upon returning from their joint bathroom break, my
dad continued telling the story of how he was once an actor
who hadn't quite made it. He blamed Mickey Rourke for
his lack of success. I was getting drunk. Xandra acted like
she never heard the story before, but clearly my father had
told it before. I blurted out, "She didn't deserve it!" They
looked at me and finally realized my drunken state.

20

By the time I arrived back at the Barbours'
apartment, I was very drunk. They exchanged knowing
glances and sent me to bed.

21

The next day I had a major headache and the smell of food was nauseating. Platt noticed my state and complained. They chastised him and he stormed off. The rest of the breakfast was practically silent.

22

My dad liked to do everything quickly and they were planning on closing up things and taking me to Las Vegas by the end of the week. The movers came quickly to clear out the apartment. Most of the stuff was sold off without any care for the items and the memories they held. There was nothing I could do except watch it happen.

23

Likewise, my days with the Barbours went all too quickly. I packed up a few boxes and labeled them for my new Las Vegas address. Andy and I wondered what it would be like in the new place as it seemed like a planet away. Neither of us was happy about the move. Despite

Mrs. Swanson and Dave's relief that I had been found a place to go, Mrs. Barbour was not as pleased.

24

Hobie put a positive spin on things by suggesting that a change of scenery might be good. I wanted to stay in the comfortable darkness of Hobie's place. He asked if I was afraid to live with my father after the stories I'd shared, but I said no. I didn't know if he'd really quit drinking or not, but I guessed he was okay.

I didn't really know how I felt about my father or his girlfriend. Hobie made sure that I had his address and phone number in case I needed it. He wished me luck and then I left, not sure if I would ever see him again.

Part Two

When we are strongest— who draws back? Most merry—
who falls down laughing? When we are very bad, — what
can they do to us? —ARTHUR RIMBAUD

Chapter Five: Boris

1

My original plan was to leave the suitcase with the painting in the package room in the care of Goldie and Jose. I felt more nervous about it as the time for me to leave drew nearer. In the end, I went back to the apartment building the day before we were to leave. When I arrived, some guy I didn't know was there and wouldn't give me the suitcase without a receipt. I tried to explain the situation, but he refused. At last, Goldie appeared and vouched for me. I thanked him for covering for me and he started talking about what was going on around there.

Before I could stop him, he was getting me a cab and putting my bag inside. I hadn't planned to take the bag with me, but then I was saying goodbye to Goldie and Jose,

who'd just arrived. It was sad to leave them and then I was
in the taxi and driving away.

2

My dad wasn't happy to see another suitcase added
to our luggage, but Mrs. Barbour had a way of convincing
him that he should be able to afford the luggage costs so
that I could have everything I needed. I thought about
leaving the bag with Mrs. Barbour and later telling her
what was in it, but in the end the bag went with me. The
goodbye was devoid of too much emotion. It was all very
polite and civil.

3

I hadn't really traveled much and had hardly been
out of the city. It was a bit of a shock to consider that I was
leaving. I was a little worried about the security check at
the airport. What if they discovered the painting? In the
back seat, my dad and Xandra were behaving disgustingly.
I was convinced then and there that they had killed my
mother even though I knew the truth.

4

At the airport, I was worried. My dad was being impatient, and I guess I looked physically ill. He told Xandra to give me a pill I hadn't known of before.

5

It was a nice pill. I felt high and happy. This feeling lasted all throughout the flight to Las Vegas. Once we got the luggage, we headed to the car. My dad was driving a nice new silver Lexus, which shocked me, given that he hadn't sent my mother any money since he left us. The pill was still working as I watched the scenery go by. I was amazed by what I saw. Xandra and my dad pointed out different highlights and aspects of Las Vegas that made it a great place. I couldn't imagine my mother there.

I asked how long my dad had had the car. He said a bit over a year. That meant that he had the car and his new girlfriend before he left us. When we got out of the Strip area and into the suburbs, I wasn't sure that we were still in Las Vegas. My dad explained that we were in a different part of the city. We kept heading away from the strip to where houses were large until we arrived at *The Ranches* at Canyon Shadows. I was impressed.

Xandra tried to explain the different building communities. My dad was busy ignoring the GPS, preferring to take a long route to the house. We finally arrived and I heard a strange sound. Xandra started yelling and picked up a small Maltese dog, Popper, who'd been left alone in the house, which now smelled like dog shit. Apparently, Xandra's friend was supposed to have walked the dog, but hadn't. The house was pretty empty, which made me think that we could have brought some of my mother's things with us.

6

I chose one of the larger rooms that were empty upstairs, but it was so bare that I hardly felt settled in. Xandra and my dad were arguing downstairs, so I sat on the mattress and took out the painting. It was the first time I had really looked at it and I was impressed. As I was taking it in, my dad knocked on the door asking if I wanted some food. I quickly put the painting in an extra pillowcase under my bed and went out.

7

There was still a few weeks left of summer before school started, so I started to learn some things. First, when my father was supposedly on business trips, he had actually been in Vegas with Xandra.

Also, my dad may have stopped drinking, but he still enjoyed a beer and Vicodin. It took me a while to sort that out as they would flash the peace sign sometimes and I never knew it meant the pill. Finally, one day they just called it what it was.

Xandra had a lot of pills around. She called them vitamins. My dad on drugs was better than my dad on booze, though, so it seemed okay. I remembered how miserable he was with me and my mom, but now he was relaxed and happy on the pills.

There was also cable TV, which we could never have before. Usually, it was on a sports channel. I wasn't sure what my dad did for work, but he seemed to be on the phone a lot. Finally, sometimes my dad and Xandra wouldn't come home at night as they stayed on the Strip since it was easier on her late days at work.

8

One day I noticed some papers on the counter and asked what they were for. Xandra explained that they were for baccarat. I had no idea what that was. She said they sometimes went to play and that Dad liked to keep track of his games. I asked if I could go sometime. She said I could except that casinos don't like kids to be around the playing. I just wanted to see the other attractions.

9

Xandra could have been someone I would have liked if I had met her as someone other than the woman who stole my father from my mother. She wasn't bad looking for her age and took care of herself. She wasn't my type either, but we managed to get along all right. I wasn't sure how she felt about me, though she complained about me a lot to her friend. She also had a way of making me feel stupid by saying "Apparently" in different tones. She worked nights and would leave in the late afternoon. When she and my dad were around I tried my best not to be.

The neighborhood was bare like the house. There weren't a lot of people around. We weren't even in a central location. There was nothing to do and no way to go places. I was used to the city with public transportation. In Las Vegas, everyone drove and I didn't yet. Luckily, we had a pool, so I spent a lot of time there with Popper.

10

School started in the middle of August. It wasn't a pleasant looking place, but on the inside it felt somewhat comforting. I was in Honors English and my classmates were a mish mash of kids. Some were military kids. Some were foreign. Some were rich kids. Many had been fairly transient in their upbringing. I jumped around from group to group, connecting on different levels with people.

Most of the kids in Honors English had a thing against Thoreau, though I didn't particularly understand. The guy who sat next to me in class didn't say much and seemed like a beggar you'd find on the streets in New York. This would be my only and best friend, Boris. We were on the same school bus together. He called me Potter because my glasses and New York style reminded him of Harry Potter. We made fun of each other and somehow started talking on the bus ride home. He lived even further out than I did so we were the last ones to get off.

Boris had an interesting story. He spoke at least four languages and had lived in a number of places in the world. His father had some important job that made him travel around the world. His mother had died many years before. I was quite impressed with his worldliness and we had similarities in our fathers' behaviors. Just as my stop was coming up, Boris asked me to go to his place and watch some TV. I wasn't sure, but he convinced me.

11

Boris' house was a 20-minute walk beyond the bus stop. Out in his area, it was even more desolated than where I was. When we got to his house, it was pretty warm and their pool was dry. Boris offered me a beer and explained that where he lived in New Guinea, they didn't have water to drink, so it was beer. He also offered me some vodka, but I didn't think it was a good idea.

We compared the preferred beverages of our fathers and hung out in his room and watched a film. Boris talked about his time in Australia. He didn't know English as well back then, so he spent his time following a woman named Judy, learning English from her conversation and music.

Time passed and Boris said he was hungry, but there was nothing to eat at his house. I suggested we go to mine since Xandra was always bringing home free food from the bar where she worked. We continued our first day of friendship together and had many more to come.

12

In New York, I had friends who were well traveled and fairly open-minded, but Boris was in a whole other league. His stories almost seemed unreal. After that first day, we were inseparable. We rode the bus together and hung out at the park smoking and talking. He was moody at times, but we managed to laugh at things and get along.

Boris told me about how he became a Muslim and then decided not to be anymore because he liked to drink. I didn't really understand. Ultimately, he said he didn't believe in anything, but the Muslims were so kind, clean and good to him that he felt like becoming one.

Sometimes Boris' English was lacking, so he would either look it up or ask me what things were or what they meant if he had never come across it before. He was behind in pop culture and things like Geography were beyond him. His father wasn't around much, so he was good on his own.

About once a week, we would walk for miles to catch a bus to a shopping plaza and steal food from the supermarket. In the Ukraine, Boris had picked pockets to get money. I'd never done that but thought we could go to the Strip since there were always drunk out-of-towners around. He didn't see the point when it was easy to steal from the store. He was also afraid of getting arrested.

It seemed the same to me: stealing food and stealing money. Boris didn't agree. To him, we were stealing food from rich corporate types. Stealing from an individual just wasn't acceptable. I tried to explain that I'd only steal from those who seemed like they weren't honest people. He countered that people who weren't honest wouldn't mind catching and killing us, or at least putting us in jail.

13

By October, Boris and I were hanging out every day. He'd drink a few beers before dinner, then have tea and eat. We'd do our homework together or talk or drink ourselves to sleep. One night I got up to go home and Boris told me not to go. We were in final parts of the movie *The Magnificent Seven*, but it was getting late. He suggested that I ask Xandra to come get me later, but I knew that wouldn't happen. They probably didn't even know I wasn't home, and Boris convinced me to finish the movie.

14

I started to miss my time at the Barbours even though I'd been grieving while I was there. Andy would write to me now and then, but he wasn't overly emotional. Mrs. Barbour sent letters regularly and it was always the same, devoid of personal feelings. Sometimes I would try to write to Pippa. Most of those letters, I never got around to sending. Boris asked if she was my girlfriend one day and if I had hit her.

He'd seen a letter where I'd apologized for her head, so he thought I must have hit her. I was offended that he thought I would hit girls. He said that maybe she deserved it. I clarified that it was unacceptable to hit women in America. He criticized America's foreign policies. One didn't have anything to do with the other, but I was bothered.

I put my energy into writing to Hobie. I tried to get information about Pippa via Hobie instead of going to her directly. Thankfully, Hobie responded promptly. I was excited when it came, but my dad grabbed it from me, wondering what it was. After he opened and inspected it, he gave it back. Hobie caught me up on life in the Village. Pippa still wasn't happy but was doing better. Hobie was going to Texas for Thanksgiving. He talked about his daily and weekly activities, ending with an offer to help me out if I ever needed anything.

15

After I got the letter, I spent the night at Boris' house. I went to bed trying to imagine Pippa and recalling stories that my mother had told me. When Boris moved, I asked him what the moon looked like in Indonesia. I wanted to know if it looked the same no matter where in the world you went. He said yes, and then asked me why. I heard a sound downstairs. His father had come home and brought along a couple of female friends. I could recognize the difference between Russian and Ukranian, thanks to Boris. They were speaking Ukrainian. After the noise settled down, we fell asleep. I dreamt of my mother telling me to go home immediately.

16

Boris' father was a mystery. He always seemed to be in some strange place or was just constantly drunk. One time I went into one of the bathrooms to find his father's suits hanging and stinking from the shower rod. It amazed me that he washed his clothes that way, but for Boris it was normal. A few weeks later, Boris showed up late to class with a shiner on his eye. He made up some excuse to the teacher that I knew wasn't true.

After class I asked what happened. "My dad happened," he said, then made an excuse for him. He worked a lot, was drunk and didn't really mean it. In the end, Boris said it was okay because his father had left him some money since he was going to be away for a few weeks. I asked if he'd reported the abuse, but he didn't see the point because he'd just get deported. We switched our focus to what we would eat that night with the money.

17

Boris had the hots for Xandra and was always drooling over her. He found out that she did cocaine by the way she behaved. I knew nothing of those things, but we came home one day and caught her doing it. Boris wanted some, but I knew that Xandra wouldn't give me anything. Boris asked how my dad paid the bills. I had no idea. I still didn't know what he did. Boris asked if there was ever cash around and I said the only thing I ever saw were chips which were perhaps just as good as cash if you were over 18 and able to cash it in. He had a point though. I had no way of fending for myself.

18

Thanksgiving came and Boris didn't have anyone to celebrate with. I didn't accept the invitation to join my dad and Xandra's romantic evening out. I did threaten to join them after Xandra started nagging at me. She looked a bit panicked. When my dad left the room, I got Xandra to stop blaming me for something my dad was doing, leaving the door open and letting mosquitoes in the house. To make peace, she offered to bring home some food from the bar to guarantee I wouldn't crash their Thanksgiving plans.

19

When I finally got to meet Boris' father, he wasn't at all what I'd expected. Since he hit Boris, I imagined a big force. Instead, he was thin and pale. He wasn't frail or weak, but his looks were deceiving. He had a bad temper and was something like a rabid fox. We met just before Thanksgiving. Boris and I came in from school, laughing and talking, when we saw him sitting in the kitchen.

We greeted each other and he took both of my hands and thanked me. He told me that I was a good person and blessed me. He said that I was like a son to him and that he was grateful that I had let Boris into my family. I was confused, but Boris translated that I was now part of their family as well. I asked afterwards what that was all about. Boris said his dad was very drunk. We hid out in Boris' room until we heard him leave.

Boris explained that his dad felt bad about leaving him alone on a holiday and had asked if Boris could stay with me. I said he did already, but he said that was why his dad had thanked me. He had given him the wrong address to my house because he was afraid that his dad would show up drunk in the middle of the night. He even told him that my last name was Potter.

20

On Thanksgiving, Boris and I were at my house eating chips, drinking vodka and watching the parade on TV. It felt like I was on another planet to see Herald Square on TV. Boris asked if my mother and I went to the parade, but I said no. There were too many tourists and stuff. I admitted to being a little bit sad. The Thanksgiving before I was with my mother, at home, celebrating and having a good time. She promised friend's place in Vermont next year. Now, that would never happen.

We took out the food that Xandra had brought home and some other stuff left in the fridge by my dad. I was already pretty close to being sick from the vodka. Boris had gone on some weird serious streak and I had to tell him to shut up because I didn't want to hear any more. We horsed around and I kept telling him to speak to me in English since he was so drunk that only Russian was coming out. We were wrestling around and the next thing I knew, I was lying near the pool doors with a pile of puke next to me.

If Boris hadn't been there, I might have cried, but I just went to the toilet to rid myself of the rest of the vodka and returned to clean up the mess I had made. I tried to remember the good times I had at the Barbours' or Hobie's house. I often managed to make myself fall asleep thinking about Hobie's workshop. I thought that I would give him a call, but no one answered and the workings of the vodka weren't yet finished. I called the Barbours, but Kitsey said they couldn't talk. They were heading out the door to a dinner somewhere. So, with a quick "Happy Thanksgiving," I was alone again.

21

After my initial encounter with Boris' father, I was less afraid of him. We crossed paths a few times and exchanged greetings, but nothing more. Then, one night we were watching a movie when the door slammed. He quickly scooped up Popper, who'd become part of our group, and shoved me out the door. I didn't know why, so I circled around to see what happened.

I saw Boris arguing with his father and suddenly his dad went crazy beating him. I couldn't believe what I was seeing. I began to run away and Boris caught up with me. His dad was shouting out the front door as we ran. I asked what happened, but Boris played it down. We went to the playground to catch our breath. Once I saw the damage that had been done, I told him we should go back to my place to clean him up. He asked for a few more minutes.

22

I admitted that it was one of the scariest things I had ever seen. Boris said his dad had killed before. We kept talking and were soon laughing again. We managed to find our way to my house and Boris was drunkenly singing in Russian. I kept kicking him, telling him to use English. We were pretty loud and tried to quiet down when we arrived at my house, but after seeing that the garage was empty, we were relieved.

I couldn't find anything decent to help clean him up and instead sprayed some perfume as an antiseptic on his face. He freaked out and hit me in the mouth. Now, I was bleeding, too. We ended up jumping into the pool, trying to get the perfume and blood off. It wasn't the best of ideas. Boris spit water at me and we began to fight in the water. He drug me under water until I felt like I was going to drown. When I surfaced Boris was trying to reach the steps out of the pool. I grabbed him and started attacking him. Finally, he told me to stop. Things had gotten out of hand, and we passed out by the pool, exhausted and drunk.

23

I woke up to the glaring sun. We were in my bed, which was damp from our wet bodies. I didn't want to move but eventually sat up. Boris groaned awake and threatened to be sick. I sent him off to the bathroom where fulfilled the threat. When he came back I was shocked by how awful he looked. He said that we were late for school. We both found this extremely funny and laughed until it hurt. Boris started getting silly and tricked me with a glass of vodka, then we were fighting again. My stomach churned and I made for the bathroom. There was another mess to greet me there. As I was berating Boris for his trick, I looked down at the pool. I told him to come over and look. It looked like a murder scene.

24

We attempted to clean up the pool and had given up on trying to go to school for the day. We rummaged around the kitchen for some food or something for the hangovers. I tried to talk to Boris about what happened with his dad, but he brushed it off like he had before. He said he knew his father loved him even if he had a bad temper.

Then, he admitted to trying to kill his father once. One winter in the Ukraine he locked his father out when he was drunk, hoping he would die in the snow. Now, he felt bad about it and was glad it hadn't happened or he'd still be stuck in the Ukraine. When I asked how he was going to explain it at school, he joked that he'd say I did it. He feared the consequences of saying anything. He would be taken away, possibly deported. He never wanted to go back there and would rather die first. I was hungry and said we should have gone to school. It was pizza that day.

25

I still carried the memory of the explosion in my body and would have dreams that woke me up. Boris never seemed bothered by my cries in the night. Sometimes he would put Popper on my chest to relax me or I would count in Spanish or Russian until I went back to sleep. At first, I would try to convince myself that my mother wasn't really dead and was waiting for me in New York somewhere. The memories started to fade along with those of the Barbours' or Hobie's home.

Hobie sent me another letter along with a book that I devoured and re-devoured. Only Boris knew the truth about my mother in Vegas and he wasn't at all surprised by the story. He'd had similar experiences of his own. Still, Boris was amazed that Hobie wrote me letters so often. He asked if Hobie was gay, but I didn't think so. Not that it would have mattered anyway. Hobie was kind and I needed kindness in my life. We all do.

26

Somehow Boris got along with my father better than I did. He would talk to my dad about the cards and baccarat he played to make money. My dad would share about his acting career , or lack thereof. He amazed Boris for some reason. I wasn't interested in anything my father had to say or anything he did, so Boris stepped in. He would come back glowing about my dad and how much he loved me and wished that it were me he was talking to instead of Boris. I didn't believe any of it.

It was still hard for me to let go of what happened between him and my mother. Boris thought I should just let it go and leave it in the past. I wasn't ready for that. My dad had won Boris over. I'd seen him do it to others before. Boris was a loyal friend, though and said he would hate him if I hated him. I didn't expect him to do that. I just warned him not to get sucked in.

27

Boris had practically moved in and although my dad was fond of him, I didn't want to draw attention to the extra drain on food and space in the house. Most of the time, Boris stayed out of the way and we hung out in my room.

Christmas was drawing close and I was feeling depressed. Boris suggested that we make our own holiday a special one and make a dinner for my father and Xandra. They seemed excited by the idea and Boris and I took a lot of time to shop and prepare for the meal.

The plan was to eat at first nightfall of Christmas Eve, but we were still cooking by around 8pm. Suddenly, my dad appeared, all decked out in a D & G suit. He suggested we get cleaned up and go out. I didn't know what to say. It was typical of him to come in and change plans at the last minute. He whined a bit and promised we could have the dinner the next day and make a new tradition of eating on Christmas day instead. He grabbed Boris to see what clothes he had that would fit him and left me with a change of plans again.

28

I rarely made it to the Strip, even though I'd moved to Vegas about six months before. Boris and I were in awe as we passed through the Venetian where my dad had made reservations. He told us to eat whatever we wanted, so we did. It was fantastic. Boris thanked him profusely and my dad said to thank the game he had bet on. He'd won a large sum of money. My dad started talking about how he won and about the dealer, Diego. He even wanted to take us back to meet him, but Xandra convinced him that Diego wouldn't be there. To change the subject, Boris raised his glass to make a toast to all of us. My father yelled out "Merry Christmas!" and gave us both stacks of twenties, $500 each. It seemed then that Christmas and happiness wasn't so impossible in this place after all.

Chapter Six: The Last Vegas Years

1

We spent most of the next year enjoying hanging out by the pool with Boris teaching me some Russian or just doing whatever we felt like doing. We were content with our camaraderie. Then, Kotku came into the scene. I can't remember her real name and Boris had given her this nickname, which is *kitty cat* in Polish.

Kotku was only a grade ahead of us in school, but was way older than us. Boris had been drawn to her for a while, but I wasn't really aware of it. Then, one day he announced that he was in love. Kotku sold weed and that's how they met. Soon, at school I saw Boris talking to a small and cute girl. It gave me a bad feeling. After school, he asked what I thought of her. I wasn't very kind in my assessment, but that somehow pleased him. He was most content that she was old enough to buy booze.

2

There was a girl in my class who I talked to sometimes named Hadley. When I asked her about Kotku, she had nothing nice to say about her. The gist was that Kotku and her mother were sluts. Kotku would do anyone and was, of course, a pot smoker and dealer. So far, I had nothing legitimate to go off of to determine why I didn't like her, but what I didn't like was that she had come into our lives and taken over Boris so quickly.

He began to be busy on Friday nights, then the weekends and soon I was finding myself alone with Popper more often than I liked. Boris couldn't help but gush over her whenever he was around. He wanted me to like her and visa versa, but I didn't know what to say. He said he was in love with her and was so happy. What could I do? He attempted to get me to go out with them or to find a date for myself, but I wasn't interested.

3

It was strange that Boris preferred Kotku when other more beautiful and more interesting girls liked him. He said he liked Kotku because she was like us. Was I really comparable to someone like her? I had fallen from being an honor student to a delinquent.

4

We still hung out, but less often, since Boris was always hanging out with Kotku and her mother. Thankfully, she hardly ever joined him at my place. Still, even if she wasn't there, Boris talked about her constantly. He tried to get us to hang out together more often, but I laughed him off. I wondered how serious they had gotten, but he half joked around. I didn't have any respect for her, having been born and raised in the area, and not knowing historical information about America. I could forgive Boris, but not Kotku. Still, there wasn't anything specific to not like about her. I just didn't like the way what Boris and I had had changed so suddenly with her presence.

I missed having him around all the time. I did the stuff we used to do together, alone. It wasn't the same. I could hang out with other crowds, but it was never as good as hanging out with Boris. Even for all the little things he did that annoyed me, he was also very giving and kind.

I had actually worried if Boris was being a bit too friendly with me. Sometimes he would embrace me in our sleep or hold me close when I had nightmares. I had some vague idea of something happening during one of our crazy drinking sessions, but I didn't have enough awareness to say for sure and we never talked about it.

I didn't want to miss him as much as I did. Things at home were getting tenser. Without Boris around to keep them in check, Xandra would drink more and slam doors. My dad was at home more and his mood swings were unbearable. He started talking about his system and why he was always watching the sports games. On Sundays he was always sitting with papers open and he was frantically making his bets from his phone.

If he won and I was around, he would share a part of his winnings with me. He was hoping it would interest me. I really didn't understand his system, but it gave us a way to connect. Sometimes I had such an overwhelming sense of sadness for my mother that I would hide out upstairs in my room. I'd listen to the music I had put on my iPod for her and look at books, mostly art ones.

I had tried to do some research on *The Goldfinch*, but I felt so paranoid at the library that I stopped looking for information about the specific painting. The painting was hidden well, or at least, I thought so. It was in a clean pillowcase duct taped to my headboard. Hobie had taught me the importance of maintaining and handling old items.

When my dad and Xandra were sure to be gone, I would sometimes take it out to look at it. I had learned a bit about the painting and the painter. Fabritius had only lived 32 years, as the son of a schoolteacher. He died in an explosion near his studio. The similarity to my experience and my mother's death was not lost on me. I compared the patterns of the painting on the wood panel to the patterns of the games my father watched. There's a point in both a sports game and looking at a painting when everything else disappears and all you are in is the moment.

5

My dad started being super nice. He was taking me out to dinner, sometimes inviting Boris who was still hanging out mostly with Kotku. The best times were when it was just the two of us. Once, my dad shared how glad he was that we were spending time together. He apologized for leaving me and not reaching out to me despite his differences with my mother. He tried to make it out as if he were the victim. I avoided pointing out how we felt.

I felt embarrassed but pleased that he was taking some responsibility. He said he wanted to make it up to me. He offered to open up a savings account for me, since he'd been doing so well, and set it aside for my future. He just needed my social security number and then he would open an account with my name on it and deposit ten thousand dollars that he already had.

6

It was already near another Thanksgiving and I hardly saw much of Boris. Then he came up one day and announced that my dad was having a bad spell. I asked for details, which Boris gave and I asked if he was sure he wasn't being conned by my dad. Boris said it was possible, but asked if I knew anything about it.

I didn't. My dad had been taking me out lately, but for the first time, Boris suggested that there may be other reasons for my dad being so kind. What other reasons? Boris didn't care to elaborate, but explained that my dad was part Russian. Most of the time, Russians complain even when things are good. However, according to Boris, my dad was different. So, what was Boris's point, I wondered? He seemed to think that my dad told him the truth of things so that I would know through him because he was too uncomfortable to tell me himself. I didn't know what to believe and figured my dad was dramatizing things for Boris. With that, Boris was off to Kotku's again, offering for me to join them. Of course, I declined.

7

Boris and Kotku's relationship quickly took on a negative quality. Although they were still physically attracted to each other, they were also constantly fighting with one another. Boris became obsessed with other men in her life with his jealousy. He also made sure that he was with her all the time at school. One day, Boris called to ask me about someone named Tyler Olowska whom I didn't know, though he was in one of my classes. Boris wanted me to find out where he lived.

As we were talking, the doorbell rang, so I told him I had to call him back. No one ever rang the doorbell and we've never had visitors before. Poppers or Popchyk, as Boris had renamed him, was going crazy. I grabbed the dog as I answered the door. Some guy with a Jersey-accent tried to calm the dog. He was a strangely dressed and weird-looking guy. He assured me that it was okay to let the dog go as he had a couple of his own at home.

He asked who I was and I gave him my name. He claimed to have recognized my New York accent, since he was from somewhere in the state. He introduced himself as Naaman Silver. I tried to be polite to him as he made small talk. Then he asked for my dad. Of course, my dad wasn't around. I didn't even know when he would be back. I offered to let him in so he could wait for my dad, but he declined. He explained that he had five points on my dad, even though I didn't know what that meant.

He didn't offer to explain, but said he didn't like to get involved with a man's home, but it was hard to find my dad lately. The phone rang again and Mr. Silver insisted I answer it. It was Boris. He wanted to know who was at the door. He was still obsessed about Kotku and began to explain that he thought she had gone home with that Tyler guy he'd asked me about. I interrupted him and said I needed to call him back.

Mr. Silver was still at the door and said he was trusting me that it hadn't been my dad on the phone. He asked me to let my dad know that he'd stopped by, making sure I knew who he was. Then, he gave some advice: "Remember kid, gambling is for tourists, not locals."

8

Boris arrived about half an hour later and I tried to tell him about Mr. Silver. He was still too preoccupied with his jealousy over Kotku. I didn't really want to talk about her anymore, but he couldn't focus on anything else. I tried to get him to not worry about it too much, and we fell into a nice silence, at last.

Then, Boris suddenly let out that he could strangle her. I was surprised. Another silence fell, but this one was more uncomfortable. Boris wasn't in the mood to watch a movie that was coming on and so he got up to leave. He said my dad was going to be the *Three Rs* if he didn't pay Mr. Silver: *revolver, roadside, or roof.*

9

I didn't know where the *Three Rs* had come from, but now I was freaked out about what it might mean for my father. A car pulled up just after dark and I was relieved to see my father. I told him about his visitor. He took it calmly and asked when. He asked if Xandra was around, but I hadn't seen her. He asked me not to mention it to her. I asked if everything was okay. He said it was and went upstairs to make some phone calls.

10

I went to my room and began to think about the painting again. I was worried and had to think of how to keep the painting safe. I couldn't think of anywhere, but decided that maybe my locker at school was the best option. It would be better to have it found by someone at school than by my dad or Mr. Silver.

I had wrapped the painting carefully, but decided to have another peek. The little yellow bird sucked me in. I pulled myself away and re-wrapped it with loads of extra tape. I put it under my sheets just in case something happened that night and drifted off to a confused and restless sleep.

11

I was tired by the time I got to school and stashed the painting in my locker. I heard someone make a comment to Kotku that drew my attention to the fact that she had a fat lip. I asked Boris if he was responsible and he shrugged that he didn't want to. She made him do it. I didn't buy that. He was defensive and I shrugged him off with my own problems to worry about. He asked about Mr. Silver. I didn't know the details of the situation. Boris said something about me getting the money for him. What did that mean? He shrugged it off and class began.

12

My dad was home early with bags from his favorite Chinese place and in a very good mood. I wanted to ask him if things had been sorted out with Mr. Silver, but Xandra was there. Since she was distracted in the kitchen, I asked if everything was ok. My father reassured me that it was fine and that there was nothing to worry about in regards to Mr. Silver. I asked what the five points meant, but he tried to explain it away without any worry. I felt relief and wanted to believe what he said was true.

13

During our bus ride to school, Boris suddenly tried to justify giving Kotku a fat lip with the time he'd done it to me. I tried to explain that it was different since he hadn't meant to hit me, but he had with her. He said he'd apologized and got upset with me again. I told him he was the one who brought it up and he laughed it off.

The night before, they had taken acid together and the experience had brought them closer. I wondered how he got it, and Boris explained that Kotku's mom had a friend who sold it to him. He was still high from it and claimed to see an aura of sadness around me. I thought he was crazy, but he was calm.

14

Things were normal for about a week, so I felt it was okay to bring the painting back to the house. When I brought it back, I noticed that it was awfully bulky, so I took it out of the pillowcase and realized I had been a bit overzealous in my wrapping. I started to try to remedy it when I heard Xandra come home. I quickly hid it behind the headboard. Boris had promised to share his last two acid drops with me. I was curious. We had done E before, but it had been a bit of a let down. We agreed that maybe over the Thanksgiving holiday we would do it.

I was feeling relaxed about things when I found my dad waiting for me after school. He said he wanted to talk to me. He started out friendly, explaining that my mom had a lawyer and that he needed me to contact him. I didn't know what he was talking about. I knew my mother had talked to someone about a divorce, or so I thought, but I wasn't really sure. Then, my dad gave me this story about how he wanted to get out of playing the books and join a partner in opening up a restaurant in Vegas. This sounded good. He said the only problem was that he needed some money. I wasn't sure what this had to do with me and the lawyer just yet.

As my father continued with his story, he gave me details about how he needed money for different restaurant taxes and insurance. I offered for my dad to use the money he said he'd set aside for me. He seemed surprised for a moment, but said that he saw an easier way. I still wasn't following. He finally got to the point. He wanted to call the number in New York and speak to someone who was my mom's lawyer. I didn't know why. My father didn't want to explain more and told me to do it just as he said to do.

I asked for more clarification, which started to test my dad's patience. He wanted me to get the lawyer to wire $65,000 to an account he had set up. I was supposed to say that I wanted to go to a private school, even though I didn't. He explained that the funds would be used for my benefit in the long run because having a restaurant would benefit everyone. His rationale was that he didn't want the government to end up taking the money due to taxes. He tried to convince me that it was in my best interests in the long run to get the money now because it wouldn't last me through college.

I wasn't convinced and hesitated. My dad was losing his cool and when I asked why I had to be the one to do it, he claimed that I knew more than I was letting on about the entire situation. I tried to say that I really didn't, but that made him angrier. I was concerned with such a large amount. Suddenly, my dad hit me hard across the face, before I knew what happened. Then, he hit me again. I was in shock. He was angry and gave me an ultimatum that I was going to do this for him whether of my own free will or by him forcing me.

I was crying by this time, from the punches more than from emotions. He tried to calm himself and apologize, but I didn't believe him. He said I just had to trust him and do it for him. As I tried to calm myself, he lost patience again, but I ignored him. He went back to trying to be reasonable again saying how we really just needed the money. I asked again whom it was that I was supposed to talk to. He explained again and tried to justify his behavior by saying how important this was to him. He promised to send me to a private school with money he made from the restaurant.

Feeling confident again about my cooperation, he dialed the number for me and gave me the phone. A woman answered and I asked for Mr. Bracegirdle and gave my name. Soon, there was a man who answered and seemed happy to hear from me. He noticed my voice was a bit strange and I said I was sick. Then, he began talking to me about how he had meant to get in touch but didn't know how. It seemed that we had met before, but I couldn't recall. He said it was a bad time and said something about a snowstorm. I remembered then that he had come by the Barbours about a week after my mother had died. He had told me about how he had met my mother. She had offered to share her cab when a snowstorm had hit the city. They worked near each other and became good friends.

My dad was listening in on another phone and he seemed on edge. Mr. Bracegirdle continued about how we had talked about my mom's estate, though I didn't remember that at all. He had wanted to talk to me, but he hadn't known how to reach me after I left New York. Watching my dad, I suddenly said that I wanted to go to private school. Mr. Bracegirdle seemed pleased with the idea and began to ask for details. We hadn't planned this far ahead and I didn't know how to respond, but he started suggesting a few possibilities. Then, my dad pushed to me to get to the point of getting the money somehow.

So, I asked and then Mr. Bracegirdle seemed a bit standoffish suddenly. He explained that my mom was having financial troubles, but had set up a UTMA for me.

This was a Uniform Transfer to Minors that was to only be used for my education while I was still a minor. I confirmed that there was no way that I could just have the money, or even some of the money, transferred to me right away. He was very emphatic that there was no way.

Mr. Bracegirdle then asked how I had come up with the specific amount of $65,000. I didn't know what to say. He quickly let it go and said there was no way for the money to be transferred. I could see that my father was horrified at what he heard. I tried to end the conversation and thanked Mr. Bracegirdle. Before we ended, he pointed out that my mother wanted to make sure that there was no way my father could touch the money. This surprised me and I wondered if he knew that my dad had put me up to this. He said that someone had tried to make a withdrawal from my account, twice. I didn't know about the account until just before the call, so I was shocked.

Mr. Bracegirdle was the custodian of the account, which meant that any activity got reported to him. Two months after my mom had died, some man had gone to the bank and forged his signature to access the money in the account. The bank knew me and called to confirm. The man disappeared before they could find out who he was.

Mr. Bracegirdle had sent a letter that I hadn't received. Someone had tried to say he was my attorney in Vegas and wanted to transfer the funds. He did some further checking only to find that someone had taken out a line of credit using my social security number. Again, I knew nothing of this information. Thankfully, Mr. Bracegirdle had shut down everything and told me to be careful about giving out my SSN. He even said I could get a new one if I needed to, but it took work. When I finally finished with the call, my father let out a howl. He was crying. I didn't know what to do, so I went to my room to drown him out.

15

According to Boris, my father told him that I had a fortune. I had no knowledge of a fortune and if I had, I would have told Boris about it. I was getting scared of my father. Boris and I were finally taking our acid hit, but I didn't feel anything. Boris told me his dad had to leave for a job in Australia in a few months and on to Russia.

I didn't know what to say to that. I couldn't imagine life without him. He said he wasn't going with him. He would run away and asked if I wanted to go with him. I immediately agreed, then checked if Kotku was also joining. He wasn't sure. In a moment of silence, the acid hit me and I felt everything in extreme intensity. It would be easy to be lost in this new sensation, but I wanted to be sure to catch what Boris was saying.

He said for Kotku it wouldn't be running away, since she'd lived on the streets before. Boris had too, in Ukraine, but not for survival. Kotku had to survive on the streets and that was why she had left school and was now back. I felt sad for Kotku and Boris and I apologized for not liking her. He said he was sorry too, but that she also didn't like me. She thought I was spoiled and hadn't had enough tough experiences. This was true.

The acid trip was starting take full effect for both of us. We were seeing the world with the effects of a black and white film. Boris wanted something in color, like Mary Poppins, which made me fall over laughing. Suddenly, the color switch went on at the same time for both of us and we continued to laugh. Through our laughter, I realized that laughter is light and light is laughter, which was the secret of the universe. We had an amazing night. I remember it as one of the best in my life.

16

Boris stayed over at my house after our evening and was at the house still when a second visit by Mr. Silver happened. We hadn't slept much, but were hanging out when the doorbell rang. Popchyk had been unsettled all night and then went crazy with the visitor.

Boris grabbed the dog and answered the door for me. Then he was back and sobered. Without a word, I got up and went to the door to find Mr. Silver there with a friend. His friend was a large man covered in tattoos on his arms and holding a metal baseball bat.

Mr. Silver was pleasant enough, asking how I was and noticing my bruised face. He asked if everything was okay between me and Dad. I didn't know how to answer him. His friend was making me uncomfortable. Mr. Silver said that if I were having any problems, he would take care of them for me. I didn't know what that meant.

Mr. Silver explained the situation. He had a big problem with my father. My father owed him 50 grand. I said that my dad was trying to get the money together and asked if maybe he could wait a little bit longer. Mr. Silver wasn't sympathetic. My dad was late in his payments and was avoiding him. His time and energy was being disrespected. He wanted me to tell my father that things could be settled reasonably if he talked to Mr. Silver to work things out. I asked what that meant. It meant that my dad needed to pay him what he was owed. If he had to pay another visit, he wouldn't be so nice.

17

When I got back to the living room, Boris was annoyed by the man with the bat. Boris said he was Russian and was just meant to scare me. How did he know? The tattoos were the giveaway. I was just dazed when Boris suggested getting out of the house. I wished my dad had been home to get what he deserved from Mr. Silver.

Boris kicked me out of my daze, turning my attention back to getting food. We decided to find some money and got ready to head out. I gave Popper some exercise and Boris and I started joking around as we pooled our money together. Suddenly, we noticed that Xandra had come in and was looking at us strangely.

We stopped talking but continued our activity. Usually Xandra wasn't home at this time, but her schedule was so strange that we weren't that surprised to see her. When she said my name cautiously, we both stopped. She never called me by my name. "Your dad's had a car accident," she said. I asked for details. He'd been drunk, of course. I wasn't shocked and asked when he was coming home. She was confused by my question. Then, she stoically said, "He died. He's dead."

18

The hours that passed after that were a blur. Xandra's friends came over. Boris shared some of Kotku's weed with everyone. Pizza was delivered, which was shocking since we had never been able to get delivery out there before. It was hard to believe that my dad wasn't coming home. He had veered into the oncoming lane just around two that afternoon. The tractor-trailer had hit him head-on and killed him instantly.

Although my dad was supposedly off the drink, I thought he might have gone back to it. Xandra was more confused about where he had the accident, just outside of Vegas, heading west into the desert. He wouldn't have gone that way without telling her first. I was surprised at her insistence that my father would have told her the truth. Boris realized that Xandra had no idea about the predicament my father was in. Recalling previous experience, it would have been no surprise if my father had stopped at a bar to build up some courage and then thought to skip town.

I never cried, but was shaken with disbelief about the whole thing. Xandra was up and down with her emotions. Boris tried to leave once since he hadn't seen or talked to Kotku in 48 hours, which was probably the longest they had ever been apart. I told him to tell her to come over, but I didn't want him to go.

Since Xandra was distracted, Boris was able to go to her room, which was always locked, to make a phone call. Kotku had told him to stay and pass on her condolences. I was surprised to hear that, but her dad had died too, so she understood. Xandra had taken one of her pills and was nearly passed out when her friends left.

Boris was the one who took care of her with another friend, Courtney. They took her upstairs and laid her down on the bed. It was my first glimpse into their bedroom since I had come to live with them in Vegas. It was a typical mess. Courtney offered to stay, more for Boris than for me, but he said he was fine. It made us both laugh.

19

Once everyone was gone, Boris and I went through the bedroom taking some of her money and checking out her stuff. It turned out that her real name *was* Sandra! Boris went through her nightstand and took a strip of condoms. Then, he found her stash of tip money. There was other stuff included in her stash. My eyes laid on a pair of diamond and emerald earrings that my mother had accused my father of stealing. I was shocked to see them and took them back for my mother.

Boris found a film canister filled with coke. He claimed you could get a lot of money for my mother's earrings. It seems Xandra had taken more of my mother's jewelry when they had come to get me. Boris suggested that I join him in his drug frenzy, but I declined the offer. I was surprised that he had done so much already, but it seemed that Kotku was a good influence in that area for him. I was busy sorting through the money.

I was focused. I needed to get out of there before anyone showed up. Boris didn't know what I was talking about. There was $1,321 plus change that I split in half for each of us. I figured we could get two tickets out of there. Boris couldn't understand why we would need to leave so soon. I explained how I had no one in the area and that the Children's Services would put me in a home to be lost in the system forever. Then, he asked about Xandra. I said it was best not to wait around until she woke up and realized we had stolen from her. Boris felt bad for her. I didn't.

My action plan was too fast for Boris. I didn't see why he was having difficulty. He had just talked about running away the night before. He asked where we would go. I said New York. He suggested California. I didn't know why. I could feel myself faltering in my conviction to go to New York, and asked him where. He didn't have a destination and just said it would be fun. We could do whatever we wanted and sleep on the beach.

I agreed, knowing that it probably wasn't a good idea. Boris was so happy that I agreed. We just had to go right away. He wasn't ready to do that. He needed more time. I knew he didn't understand about the Children's Services, so I gave him an ultimatum. He said he would come, but he needed a day. I knew why. He wanted to see Kotku first. He tried to convince me to stay over at his place and wait. There was no way that I could wait.

Boris got serious suddenly and said that there was something important he had to tell me. He said it meant that I needed to stay and that I was making a mistake. I had lost my patience at this point. I got the painting in its pillowcase and packed up my overnight bag. I grabbed my school jacket because I had nothing else warm and it would be cold in New York.

Boris asked where I was going to go. I said I would go back to the Barbours. He tried to convince me that if they had wanted me they would have adopted me already. I explained they couldn't have since my father returned. He again tried to tell me they didn't want me, but I knew it wasn't true. He threw out every possible reason he could, but I told him to leave me alone.

I headed downstairs and Popper stopped, staring at us confused. I didn't know what to do with him. Boris couldn't take him, so I snatched him and took the dog with me out the door. I didn't want to leave him there to be mistreated by Xandra.

Boris asked where I was going. I said to the airport. Then, I realized that maybe I couldn't go with the dog. Perhaps I could take a train instead. Just as he was going to say something, Boris looked and I turned to see Xandra looking a mess at the top of the staircase. She asked about some keys to the bank vault and then Boris told her to go back to bed. She mumbled and turned away.

We quickly got out of the house. It seemed to snap Boris out a bit and I asked him for his phone. I called a car to pick me up. He told me to keep the phone, but I didn't want it. He tried again to get me to stay, but I wouldn't budge. I wasn't sure if I would ever see him again. I asked him to meet me in a day or two. He could just take a plane and I would tell him where I was at. I asked him not to say no and he said he wouldn't but it was the same as saying no. I was exhausted. Boris offered me more drugs. I refused at first, but he convinced me that it would clear me up. I took a sniff as directed and was instantly clearer. Boris said he planned to sell the stuff since you could get good money for it. It turns out he was hanging out with more people than I never imagined.

I was still trying to convince Boris to come out to New York with the things that we could do together out there. I offered to give him some of my money for school. As I kept babbling, Boris put his hands on my face and kissed me. He picked up Popper and kissed him, then handed the dog to me. The car had arrived.

"Good luck. I won't forget you," he said. Then, I was in the cab and heading away. I wanted to convince him to come just one more time, knowing that if the moment had been just right, he might have agreed. I didn't and probably it was for the best. I was relieved that I hadn't blurted out what I wanted to say most, *I love you*.

20

The cab driver figured out that something was wrong and tried to give me a number for the National Runaway switchboard, but I didn't take it. I just asked him to take me to the train station. He told me that dogs weren't allowed on the train. I didn't know what to do. He said maybe on the plane, but I would need some kind of case for him. He suggested the bus as the best option, but he didn't think they let underage kids ride alone.

I explained that my dad died and his girlfriend was sending me back east to my family. I was silent for the rest of the ride letting the reality of my dad's death sink in. In New York, people didn't really have to worry about drunk driving. I wondered what would happen to his body.

Andy and I had scattered my mom's ashes in Central Park even though it was against the rules. We arrived at the Greyhound bus station and the taxi driver gave me some advice about Popper. He suggested I put him in a bag to carry on because it wasn't likely that he was going to be allowed on the bus either.

My bag was kind of big and he thought I might have to put it in the luggage area anyway. So, he found a large canvas shopping bag in his trunk that would fit the dog just right. He offered to wait with Popper until I got my ticket. The driver was right about not being able to take the bus as an unaccompanied minor. The rule was for children under 15. Fortunately, I was 15 and convinced the ticket lady that I was old enough by showing her my ID. Enrique had suggested I get one when they were going to put me into the system. I was glad that I had it.

The lady gave in and I noticed a sign that said no animals were allowed on the bus. I managed to have arrived just in time for a bus that was departing in fifteen minutes and wondered what I should do with the dog. I thought maybe the driver would take him or something might happen to him. The driver found a way to conceal him well in the bag and he gave me some tips for how to keep him hidden on the journey.

21

Our first stop was in Colorado, after passing through Utah. I hadn't been able to sleep, but luckily I had been able to keep my bag with me and Popper had not been noticed so far. At the 50-minute stop, I let Popper get some exercise out of sight of the driver and bought some food for both of us. On the bus again, I managed to get some sleep. We repeated this again at each stop passing through Missouri, the area where my mother had grown up.

We had to change buses in St. Louis. About an hour or two after we set off, I woke up to find the bus had stopped. The driver was standing over me telling me I could not have the dog on the bus. I didn't know what to do. She asked if anyone else on the bus had a problem with the dog on the bus. No one did. She let it pass and warned that if someone complained, I would have to get off.

I agreed to her terms with some surprise and relief. I was rattled now, thinking that if I had to get off the bus I would be stranded in the middle of nowhere. It seemed silly that I had become so attached to a little dog. After that, I was afraid to fall asleep again, so I watched the scenery pass, thinking about my mother. Eventually, I dozed off until Cleveland where we made another transfer. As we neared the city, I felt sick and it hit me full on when we arrived in Port Authority.

I quickly went outside and knew that I must look a mess after an over 60-hour bus journey. When we got out, I thought Popper would feel relief to be able to walk, but instead he was frightened by everything. He calmed again once I picked him and put him safely back in the bag.

My hunger drove me to the first place I could find, which was a cupcake place. Once I'd devoured a cupcake and the sugar hit, I felt better and started to rethink what my plan of action was. I wasn't sure what Mrs. Barbour would do. Would she call Social Services? What would she think of Popper, especially since Andy was allergic to everything? Still wondering, I began to walk toward Park Avenue. When I arrived at Central Park, I felt a mix of feelings. It was soothing to be among the trees, yet it felt haunted with the ghost of my mother.

As I continued on, I saw a familiar man pass me. It could only be Mr. Barbour on his way home from work. I ran up to him, but he was mumbling to himself. I called again and said it was Theo, grabbing his arm. He violently threw my hand off and looked at me without recognition. He told me to get lost. I should have known what mania was, after spending time with my dad, but I'd never seen Mr. Barbour this way before. I withdrew in shame. He glared at me and then marched off.

I ran back into the park near the Pond and instinctively headed to the Rendezvous Point. It was the place where my mother and I had sat. The exchange with Mr. Barbour had shaken me. I had expected a warm welcome and that he'd take me home.

I didn't know what I should do. As I tried to figure something out, I happily saw that I had a text from Boris. He said he hoped we were ok and that I should get in touch with Xandra. I tried to call him, but no one answered. I would deal with Xandra later. I began to think that I would have to stay on the street and it was cold. I supposed I could call Andy and see if he would meet me and at least bring me some clothes or something. But it had been nearly two years since I'd seen him and I was still disturbed by Mr. Barbour's reaction on the street.

While I was thinking, a man started talking to me, which frightened me. I got up to go. He grabbed my wrist and then I twisted free and ran. I had forgotten about the dangers and life of New York. I was still feeling sick, but walked to loosen up from the bus ride. Finally, I was too cold and got a cab to take me to the Village.

It wasn't ideal for me to show up at Hobie's since we hadn't been in touch for a while. I felt so awful, though, and had nowhere else to turn. When I arrived, it looked as if the shop hadn't been opened since I left. I hesitated to ring the bell, but eventually I did, not knowing any other options. The door was opened by a girl my own age.

It was Pippa. She looked healthier since I'd last seen her and a bit different. I must have looked different to her as well because she asked if she could help me at the door. Just then, Hobie appeared and at first I thought he didn't recognize me either. I quickly said, "It's me, Theodore Decker."

Pippa recognized my name, but they were so surprised at how I looked that I began to cry. Hobie hugged me and took me inside, asking questions like, "When did you get back?" and "Are you hungry?" Popper popped his head out and Pippa was so happy to see the little dog that I finally felt relief that they had let me inside.

In the kitchen, Hobie gave me some mushroom soup, which helped to warm me up. I explained briefly what had happened. Hobie said I had to call Xandra to let her know that I was okay. I didn't want to, but he insisted that it was the right thing to do and to do it right away. She was the last person I wanted to talk to, but Hobie insisted. I dialed her number hoping she wouldn't pick up.

She answered on the first ring and accused me of leaving the door open and letting the dog run away. I said he was with me. She sounded relieved at that at least. Then, she asked where I was at. She assumed with Boris. I said no to that as well, though she had talked to Boris. She threatened that she should call the cops for all the money I had taken. Then, I accused her of stealing my mother's earrings, but she claimed my father had given them to her.

The conversation wasn't going anywhere productive. In the end, she said that I was heading down a bad path and so was Boris. She was giving me a heads up based on her own experience and knowledge of the world. She said she loved my dad, but that he wasn't the greatest man and probably neither was my mother. The last comment made me mad. I said I would hang up.

She apologized for including my mother and then told me that she was having my dad cremated. I didn't care. She asked for an address so she could get in touch with me. I told her it was unlikely that would ever be necessary and she insisted on having a contact. I told her to get in touch with my lawyer, George Bracegirdle. I said she could look the number up herself.

Xandra continued on, commenting that I wasn't responding to my father's death like a normal son. I told her that my feelings for him were probably exactly what he felt for me. She told me we were more alike than I thought. This upset me again. I contemplated her statement as I tried to sleep in Hobie's spare room. It wasn't true. Still, I heard her words throughout my dreams.

Part Three

We are so accustomed to disguise ourselves to others, that in the end, we become disguised to ourselves. —
FRANÇOIS DE LA ROCHEFOUCAULD

Chapter Seven: Returning to New York

1

For a while, I just laid in the bed, taking in my surroundings. I finally sat up after having a sneezing fit and checked under the bed to make sure that the pillowcase with the painting was still there. I went to the bathroom where I saw that my hair was such a mess that a comb wouldn't go through it. I sawed it off with some rusted nail scissors. I realized then why I had been unrecognizable, with a bruised jaw, acne-covered chin, swollen eyes and being sick. It would be easy to misjudge me as some escapee from a cult or something.

It was 9am and I could hear a morning classical program playing on the radio. Hobie was in the kitchen with a book that he wasn't reading. He was dressed for the workshop and greeted me with a start. When I tried to talk, my voice was rough. Hobie poured me some tea and put a plate of food in front of me. I was still a mess and spilled the tea when I grabbed for it. I blurted out that I was sorry. He seemed confused.

"Please don't make me go," I said.

"Make you go? Go where?" he asked. He said the only place he would make me go is back to bed because I sounded so bad. I wasn't convinced of his sincerity and stared at where his old dog, Cosmo, used to sleep. Hobie noticed the direction of my eyes and explained that Cosmo had died. I said nothing.

He tried to reassure me that everything was okay now, but I told him I had nowhere to go. He asked my age and what had happened about my grandfather. I said I hadn't spoken to him directly. Xandra's friend called him to tell him about my dad, and he didn't seem to be bothered. He just thanked her for letting him know and that was it. I explained that my grandpa and his wife hadn't liked my father that much and hadn't had anything to do with him or me. I was talking fast, trying to explain.

Hobie told me to calm down and that he was just wanted to understand the situation. I told him about Mr. Bracegirdle and asked if he would go with me to see him. Pippa came back in from outside, asking what was wrong with the dog since he had been so freaked out by the cars outside. She was happy with Popchyk, saying she loved dogs and had studied about all the different breeds.

I began to sneeze again. Hobie sent me back to bed and asked what I wanted for breakfast. I said anything was fine. He said he would make me oatmeal since it would be good for my throat. He asked if I had any socks or pajamas, neither of which I had. He found some things of Welty's and put his hand on my shoulder, which made me jump. He told me I could stay as long as I liked and not to worry about it. He agreed to go with me to see the lawyer. He said everything would be fine.

2

I made it back to the room and through my feverish dreams, I was comforted by Hobie's voice, Welty's aura and Pippa's presence. Still, throughout it all, I saw yellow feathers, a flash of crimson and bright black eyes.

I was startled awake, dreaming of someone trying to take the painting, to find Pippa taking the dog out. She told me not to sneeze on her. I apologized and said I was feeling better. She asked if I was bored and would like her to bring me some colored pencils. I was confused by the offer and she was offended. She went out and Popchyk followed. I was worried that the drugs had messed up my brain and nervous system as I berated myself for my stupidity in my response to her offer.

My phone beeped with a message from Boris. He was at the MGM grand. We texted back and forth a bit. Then, Hobie stuck his head in, asking if I needed anything. I said I was okay. He asked me to let him know when I was hungry because there were loads of leftovers from their Thanksgiving dinner a few days before. Boris was still sending me texts when Hobie went out. I told him to call me later, but there was no response. It was to be a long time before I heard from him again.

3

For the next few days, I struggled in bed with flashbacks in my dreams of Port Authority or Vegas. Time passed without me knowing anything. Hobie would bring me aspirin, ginger ale and ice. Popchyk would jump around at the foot of the bed, all nice and clean. Pippa told me to move over so she could sit on the bed next to me. I was having a dream about the painting which showed on my face. She asked what was wrong and I said nothing. She handed me a green origami she made. It was a frog, meant to jump when you pushed on the backside.

She saw my iPod and grabbed it, asking if she could look at it. As she scrolled through the music, she would say nice and read artists. She asked if I had any classical. I said some, but it had mostly been my mother's stuff on the iPod. She offered to make me some CDs. I tried to talk to her, but it wasn't the same as it had been before. She watched me and began laughing, wondering why I was looking her in such a way. I wasn't sure what that way was, but I guess I was too serious and intense.

Did she have nightmares about what happened? Did she have fears and flashbacks related to the accident? I wanted to ask her, but I knew I couldn't. She had a hysterical kind of laugh that reminded me of my times with Boris and I connected it to a near death experience.

4

On Monday, I forced myself out of bed to call Mr. Bracegirdle's office. His secretary seemed a bit hesitant to connect me when I said who I was and told me he was out. She asked for a number. I gave her Hobie's number and regretted not making an appointment to see him after I hung up. Soon after I got off the phone, he rang back.

He noticed the New York area code, and I said I'd left Vegas. He asked what he could do for me. I explained what had happened and he gave his condolences. While I filled him in, he listened quietly. He said he felt more comfortable talking to me freely now. It seemed that no one had known what to do when my father showed up. My mother and Mrs. Barbour had all expressed concerns about my father, but it was a difficult situation when he came back. He said the last time we spoke, he sensed a rat when I quoted the specific amount of money. He had lied about being unable to withdraw money. I was confused, but understood that I did have access to the money.

This news hit me hard as I could have been in a very different position right now had he told me the truth before. He clarified that there wasn't actually $65,000 in the account, but it was there and growing all the time. He suggested we could work out a way for me to get some of it now. He also said it was wise of me to have returned to the city on my own. He had to go, but asked where I was staying. I told him with friends in the Village. He gave me over to his secretary to set up an appointment. When I got off the phone I felt sick. Hobie asked if I was okay and I just shrugged, "Sure." Back in my room, I began to cry as Popchyk tried to console me.

5

Although I had been starting to feel better, this news set me back again and my fever returned. My dad was all I could think of. I kept thinking that I had to call him as if he hadn't died after all. Then, I dreamt of him berating me for a small mistake. It was then that I became aware of a light in the hallway and a shadow at my door.

Pippa was standing there, unsure about waking me. I was half awake and told her to wait. I put on my glasses and noticed that she was ready to go out. She was about to leave and wanted to say good-bye. She had to return to boarding school and wasn't sure when she would be able to visit again. I still didn't comprehend, thinking I would see her again soon. We talked a bit and she had to go.

Her presence had been noted all throughout the days, even though I'd been sick in bed. I thought of all the nice things we could do once I was feeling better, but now that wasn't going to happen. Hobie said they had to go and then she said goodbye.

I watched them walk away down the street from the window. I went to her room and saw that it hadn't changed much since the last time I'd been in it. It smelled like her and I felt so happy to take in her essence in the room. As I looked around, I noticed a buzzing noise. I thought it was someone coming. Instead, I found Popchyk snuggled in her pillow, fresh from a bath. I crawled into the bed with him and fell into a happy sleep surrounded in her scent.

6

When I finally met Mr. Bracegirdle, he commented that I looked like my mother, but I knew that I looked much more like my father. Mr. Bracegirdle and Hobie talked quietly. Mr. Bracegirdle was telling him how he'd met my mother and was getting to know more about Hobie. As they spoke, I was surprised to find that Mr. Bracegirdle had known a lot more about my mother than I realized. It made sense as I noticed all the art books he had in his office.

They turned their attention back to me. Mr. Bracegirdle explained that I was now old enough that a judge would probably grant my wish about my guardianship and living conditions. In the meantime, he supposed I could be given temporary guardianship elsewhere, but he didn't see it as necessary as long I was content with the situation. Hobie agreed that he was happy with things. Then, Mr. Bracegirdle brought up the issue of my schooling. Although we had talked about boarding school before, he suggested it probably wasn't such a great idea to send me off anywhere right away, since the winter holidays were coming. He offered to be contacted anytime, day or night, at home or at work, if necessary.

He asked if this was definitely what I wanted and clarified that I would stay with Hobie for the next few weeks. This unsettled me, but I said yes. He said that I could go to a boarding school and they could find a family for me to stay with over the holidays. I felt as if that was what they were encouraging me to do. I just stared at my shoes. They decided that as long as I was happy with staying at Hobie's, that would be fine. With that, he told me to think about what I wanted to do about school.

7

I wasn't happy with the sense of temporariness in guardianship and with where I was staying. I decided to focus on my application to enter an early-college program in the city in hopes that it would give me more permanence. Most days I would spend in my room, studying for the tests. I worked like I was punishing myself for not living up to expectations, lately. The work was good for me, too, in that I was too focused and drained to obsess over my shame and guilt over my situation.

The issue with the painting was always in the back of my mind. It would be crazy to confide in Mr. Bracegirdle. He already wanted to send me off to boarding school. Hobie was still always an option, but I could never come up with a suitable scenario of how things would play out once I told him. Like my guilt over the death of my mother, I felt the same about my father's death. Of course, I couldn't have done anything to help him out of his troubles exactly, but I still felt responsible, especially since Mr. Bracegirdle had lied to me about my money.

Pippa's absence was noticed. Everything was quiet, now. I would wonder about her a lot, to the point of almost being obsessed. I really missed her presence. Still, I liked the safety and enclosure that the house offered. Hobie's presence down in the workshop was my anchor and my comfort. Before, I hadn't had my own money for things and it was awkward for me to ask for it from the Barbours. With my living stipend from Mr. Bracegirdle, I was able to pay for Popchyk's vet bills, take care of my dental needs, buy a laptop and phone as well as some clothes. I would buy groceries now and then, since Hobie wouldn't accept money for it. It was nice to be able to buy him a few treats now and then, too.

It was so easy to live with Hobie. We built our own routine together. He was so gentle towards me and would ask for my help when he needed it. From time to time, Hobie would open the shop by appointment. This usually meant a visit with friends over a bottle of sherry. I never saw him actually sell anything. Most of the time, he worked in the "hospital" downstairs, doing repairs with his old-school technology. When he finished his work for the day, he would pour himself a whiskey. Then, he would clean up and we would share dinner.

Dinner was the best time of the day. Hobie's whole day revolved around dinner. Sometimes we had people over or he cooked or we went out. Sundays often found us with guests who were professors, society ladies or other people he'd been close to over the years. While I was always present, I didn't always know what was being spoken of. The gatherings were in contrast to those at the Barbours' house. Everything was very informal.

I felt bad about not calling Andy or the Barbours since returning to the city. I didn't know what to think after my encounter with Mr. Barbour. I tried to forget the details of the state I was in when I arrived. Hobie never mentioned it when I was around, but I know that he told people about how we had met and how I'd come back. Sometimes they would talk about Welty and the way that he loved talking to people and people liked talking to him. One of Hobie's good friends, Mrs. DeFrees told me that Welty had known exactly what he was doing when he sent me to Hobie. This made me feel weird since still no one knew that Welty had given me anything more than the ring.

8

I had taken over Welty's room. At night, I would lie there, listening to the noises outside and worrying about the painting. If Hobie found it, he would know what it was and want to know why I had it. I would double-check it under the bed, but then not want to touch it anymore. I worried about a fire or an exterminator visit. If someone tried to connect the dots, they would know I was in the same room as the missing painting, and the proof was Welty's ring. Out of fear that Hobie would try to come clean the room, I was obsessive about keeping dust away.

Most days when we were home, I would stay in my room. I went out with Hobie when he went. I tried to be nonchalant about accompanying him out, but I was anxious about not losing him, similar to Popchyk not wanting to be left alone. Most of the time, I was bored with the various social engagements I accompanied Hobie to, but some things were also interesting. We were regular visitors with Mrs. DeFrees and she would comment on my social awareness. Once, at a café, the counterman asked if my dad wanted another espresso when Hobie had gone to use the restroom. I said, "No thanks," and felt pleased that people thought Hobie was my father. He was old enough to be my grandfather, but he had a European air about him that made it seem possible that he could still be my father.

I wondered why my mother hadn't found someone more like Hobie or even Mr. Bracegirdle instead of my dad. She had deserved better. Even though I wanted to forget everything I could about my father, I never really could. I was reminded of him when I looked in the mirror.

9

I took my early college program tests in January. One had seemed easy and the other quite hard. There were questions I didn't expect, so I had no idea what my chances of passing were. I asked myself what I would do should I not pass, since they only took the top 30%. I knew that I couldn't handle going to the boarding school that Mr. Bracegirdle talked about. I didn't know what other options I had. I should have probably considered a decent high school in the city, but Mr. Bracegirdle was quite insistent that I should go to a boarding school where there were so many other opportunities.

He told me that my mother would have wanted a fresh start for me, out of the city. He may have been right, but the circumstances since he'd known her had been so drastically altered that I didn't see how her wishes could stand up. I wasn't sure. I was about to go into the subway station when I noticed a headline that some masterworks from the museum had been recovered in Bronx.

I stopped and bought a copy of the newspaper and sat on a bench to read through it. It seems that a paramedic who had arrived on the scene had removed the paintings from the wall when they had been told to evacuate. The paintings had been wrapped in tinfoil in the attack of the paramedic's mother-in-law's home. She claimed to have no idea that they were there. The penalty, if found guilty, could be up to 20 years in prison.

The paramedic and his brother hadn't known anything about art and they began to do some research on the pieces they'd taken at random. They found that they couldn't sell the famous pieces, but that some of the lesser ones could be sold. This is what the investigators had picked up on. Now, the police and FBI art crimes unit believed that it was possible that there may be more of the missing masterpieces still in the city, under their noses.

I felt sick after reading the article. They were promising to prosecute for full penalties should they find any more of the missing pieces. Hobie was disturbed by the news and at the audacity of the paramedic to take the paintings off the walls while people were bleeding and injured around him. Mr. Amstiss, one of the night's guests said that he wasn't surprised that 'the help' don't know how to behave properly.

Hobie defended the role of paramedics, telling the story of when Juliet, Pippa's mother, had been sick and how well they had taken care of her. I was distracted by the conversation and Hobie asked if I was alright. I just said that I was tired, which they attributed to worrying about the tests. I said I wasn't, but they started talking about how they felt sure that I would get in.

Mr. Amstiss commented that most of the early-college programs didn't deserve the name they were given. Rather, it was a lot of hard work to get in, but once in, it was fairly easy to get through. That night, after everyone had gone and we were in for the night, I panicked. The entire world was covering the story. There were huge fines on top of the prison sentences for these crimes. I figured that if the mother-in-law who claimed to have not known a thing could be prosecuted as well, then I was also putting

Hobie in danger. There was no way anyone would believe he didn't know given the area he worked in, antiques.

My thoughts jumped all over the place and I finally took two different kinds of the pills I had taken from Xandra's to calm me down. I didn't know what the pills were, but I hoped they would work. From my research online, I learned that stolen paintings were hardly ever discovered until someone tried to sell it. Only 20% of art thieves were ever caught because of this.

Chapter Eight: Joining Hobie's World

1

I was so worried about the painting that the arrival of the letter saying I'd been accepted for the spring term to start in the early college program just left me shocked. Hobie was happy for me and I felt bad that he was so happy. We had a celebratory dinner with Mrs. DeFrees at a neighborhood Italian restaurant and I felt numb. Hobie toasted me and said I could relax a bit. He bragged to his friends about how hard I worked. Mrs. DeFrees told me to look happier and asked when I started.

2

The good news was that Mr. Amstiss wasn't so wrong in that getting in was the hard part. The actual classes and work were easier than I had ever had before. There were no requirements, in general. With no tests, exams or grades, the focus of the work was on doing projects or attending seminars. I was free to choose whatever I wanted for electives. The work involved some take-home essay questions at midterm and then a final project. Though I knew how lucky I was, I still wasn't happy about how things had turned out for me. I just did what I had to do. I showed up, doing the minimum.

Due to my extreme anxiety over the painting I wasn't sleeping well and was always jumpy. My counselor tried to get me more involved so that I would stay anchored within an urban school campus. It was lonely at school as the older kids didn't socialize with the younger ones and most kids had had sheltered lives. I had very little in common with them. She suggested that I join the French club, which was pretty active. The cinema teacher suggested the Cinema club or the Philosophy Club. I wasn't drawn to anything.

Eventually, the teachers started to give up on my lack of interest in challenging and developing myself beyond what I had to do. In fact, it seemed that most of the teachers started to resent me for not taking advantage of the opportunities provided for me. I began to wonder if I had been allowed into the program based on my tragic life or actually passing the exams. I started to feel bad that I had probably taken the place of some other more deserving kid who would have taken advantage of all that was available through the program.

My reports were never stellar, as the teachers commented that I never did more than I had to. Despite this, I was not motivated to do more or to prove myself to anyone. Instead, I would ride the subway to the end of their lines and walk around the neighborhoods alone. Soon, even the train rides bored me, so I began to bury myself in Hobie's basement for hours.

Eventually, I developed a numbed way of life where the past ones started to fade from memory. Occasionally, at unknown times, something would remind me of the way I used to be and I would recall Boris. I had long ago given up contacting him and had no idea what he was doing now. Sometimes I would have a memory of my father that

caused a severe pain. Once when that happened I bought
Chinese take out, much to Hobie's surprise.

3

We still hadn't clarified my status at Hobie's home.
Mr. Bracegirdle still seemed to think it was temporary, with
an occasional chat with me about how they could possibly
find a place for me in the dorm at college. I never engaged
in the conversation when he brought it up, so he would
leave it alone. With my constant anxiety, I worked hard to
be indispensable to Hobie by running errands, cleaning his
tools or helping with things around the workshop. As I
helped, I learned more about the restoration of items.

4

Time started to pass without notice from me. I
would read at night, learning about art and antiques.
Sometimes I would work long hours with Hobie. It was
always relaxing to work with Hobie. I was never lonely
with him and he continued to talk to me as an equal,
explaining the various aspects of restoring furniture and the
tools. It was the happiest place for me.

5

I continued to follow the news about the art thieves who'd been caught. They plead guilty and received huge fines and full prison sentences. If they hadn't tried to sell the paintings to a dealer who called the police, they still might be free. One day I had returned from school to find the upstairs in smoke and firemen in the hall outside the bedroom. Hobie said mice had chewed through the electrical wires. He meant to get an exterminator in and didn't like the glue traps, but now he was convinced that something needed to be done. If the alarm hadn't gone off, then the place would have gone up in flames.

Luckily, only the floorboards in the hall had been damaged, but I was shaken by the incident. What if Hobie hadn't been home? What if the fire had started in my room? I thought I should set my own traps or suggest that Hobie get a cat. When I did suggest it, he and Mrs. DeFrees thought it was a good idea, but it never happened.

A few weeks later, I found Hobie kneeling on a rug in front of my bed. I thought he was reaching under my bed, but he had just bent to pick up a putty knife. He was replacing a cracked pane at the bottom of the window. He greeted me and explained what he was doing. I was so relieved and knew that I was acting a little crazy. I still didn't know what to do. I was always so jumpy and worried that something would happen.

Finally, after about eight months with Hobie, a solution presented itself. Hobie had a few guys who worked for him over to move items from the shop to a storage unit. I was on pretty good terms with all of them. One day, Grisha, a Russian Jew, stopped by to drop off some furniture and I was alone in the house. I helped him to unload the furniture for Hobie to work on. He asked if I had time to help him in the afternoon too since one the guys was sick that day.

6

In a van full of furniture, on our way to Brooklyn, Grisha talked non-stop about how Hobie was really a great man, but that he was running the business into the ground. Grisha said that Hobie was an artist and did amazing work, but he was by no means a businessman. For example, Hobie was paying for a storage unit out in Brooklyn Navy

Yard, instead of moving inventory and paying the bills. The items kept coming in, but nothing was going out.

Grisha pointed out that there was a ton of money to be made, but it wasn't happening. I tried to say that Hobie had sold some stuff just the previous week, but Grisha didn't like the Vogels, the buyers. They claimed they were taking advantage of Hobie. Grisha ranted that he loved Hobie, but that if things kept going the way they were, he would be broke in four to five years. Grisha said Hobie needed to find someone to run the shop for him. I asked who. Grisha told me about his cousin who could sell anything to anyone. I suggested that Grisha tell Hobie and maybe he would hire Grisha's cousin. Grisha laughed and said no way would she work for Hobie. He was just saying that Hobie needed someone like her.

We had arrived at the storage place and as Grisha signed in, I looked at a brochure. The brochure was advertising a storage facility for fine arts. We loaded up the elevator and took the furniture to the unit, which was already packed to the gills with stuff. I felt disoriented by all of the stuff that was there. Grisha said that Hobie paid $2,000 a month for the unit. I asked how much the smaller units went for and Grisha said it was crazy at hundreds of dollars a month for a small space. I asked how anyone would know if people stored illegal stuff in the units. He confirmed there was nothing to stop anyone from doing that, as most likely no one would ever find it. He hated the place with everything all shut up in a metal box.

7

When I got back that night, I looked in the Yellow Pages for a storage facility that specialized in fine arts. There were quite a few in the area, but they all seemed to offer too much for my needs. Then, I found a place that looked good and was near my old neighborhood. The next day I skipped class and took the pillow-cased painting in a bag with me. On the way, I stopped to pick up a tent and headed to the storage facility.

It was pretty easy to pay cash for a year in advance for a locker. I memorized the locker number and combination and felt such a huge relief to have the safety of the painting off my shoulders. Since I was in my old area, I thought I would walk over to our old building and see the door guys again. It would be nice to see them and catch up.

Ss I got halfway down the block from the building, I saw scaffolding and the building in disarray. I was shocked and dismayed to find it was being destroyed. I asked a guy working on deconstructing the building what happened, explaining that I used to live there. He said the owners had sold the place and they were replacing it with upscale condos. All of my old memories were gone. I kept walking, more and more distraught that everything I had in connection to my parents was now gone forever.

Part Four

It is not flesh and blood, but heart which makes us fathers and sons. - SCHILLER

Chapter Nine: Settling in to Life

1

Eight years passed. I'd stopped going to school and was working for Hobie. I had just come out of the Bank of New York when I heard my name. As I turned, I saw someone I didn't recognize, even though the voice was familiar. "It's Platt, Platt Barbour," the man said.

I was amazed. He looked very different, but I greeted him, wondering how he was doing. Platt said he was in the city and had just started a new job with an academic publisher. I didn't know what to say to him and asked about Andy. At that question, his face dropped and he said, "You don't know?"

In all these years, I still had not reached out to Andy. I had heard about him and knew that he had gone to MIT, but that was it.

"He's dead," Platt continued, "and daddy too." I couldn't believe it. I was stunned. Platt went on to explain that Andy and Mr. Barbour had drowned about five months ago. It seemed so hard to believe. The news physically shook me. Platt suggested that we get a drink nearby.

2

In the bar, Platt rambled on about what happened. His father had been getting worse with his mental state. Although the kids had been fairly sheltered from it when they were young, as they got older, they realized just how bad Mr. Barbour was. He started to decline again a few years ago by having public outbursts and making strange calls. He had gone back to the hospital, but when he came back this second time he wasn't the same.

His ups and downs were less extreme, but he couldn't concentrate and was irritable. A month or so before the accident, he changed doctors, took a leave of absence from his job and went to Maine to stay at Platt's uncle's place. Mr. Barbour had always felt solace being near the sea. The family took turns to visit him, but since Andy was the closest, at MIT in Boston, he got stuck dealing with his father the most.

Mr. Barbour refused to go back to an institution and the best they could do was help with his medication and hope he would be okay. The doctor said it was fine for him to do most things, if he wanted.

Mr. Barbour wanted to go sailing. It was late in the day, but since Mr. Barbour was so comfortable on the water, they went out. Platt asked Andy to come help as he'd been out partying the night before. When Mr. Barbour decided he wanted to go out for a sail, it all seemed fine. They hadn't gone out very far, but Platt hadn't paid attention to the weather. When the wind picked up, Mr. Barbour fell overboard. Platt and Andy tried to help him back in, but a big swell caught them and capsized the boat. The water was freezing and Mr. Barbour caught hypothermia, in the water for an hour and a half. Andy somehow lost his life jacket in and had drowned.

It was a shocking tale. Platt had always been such an ass to Andy and the memories came back. Platt finally stopped talking and said I should go see his mother. He meant right then, which startled me. He pleaded and as I looked at my watch, I realized that the drink had set me off course from the errands I meant to do that afternoon. Platt asked again, just for a minute.

3

It was a time warp to step back into the foyer of the familiar apartment. When I went towards the living room, Platt corrected me saying that now his mother greeted people in her bedroom area in the back. It seemed she had drastically slimmed down her social life after the death of Andy and her husband. Platt knocked on her door, "Mommy? I've got a guest for you. You'll never guess…"

As I leaned in, she recognized me right away and seemed very pleased to see me. She had greatly changed, but still had elegance about her. She marveled at how I had grown and asked where I had been. I took a seat in an armchair by her bed and paused a moment as memories flooded back. Mrs. Barbour offered me a cup of tea or something to drink, which I politely declined.

She patted the side of the bed to invite me to come closer so she could see me better. I expressed my surprise, sadness and condolences. She was quiet, trying not to cry and all I could think to do was hold her hand. She broke the silence after a few moments and started talking about Andy. He had mentioned me just a few days before his death. He had gotten engaged to a Japanese girl. That wasn't surprising, since Andy had chosen to take Japanese due to his fetish with the girls.

Mrs. Barbour turned her attention to her two little dogs that kept her company on her bed. She said she was considering a third dog as they had been a major comfort to her during this time. Since Andy had been so allergic, she couldn't have had animals before, but now….

Platt had returned and he and his mother exchanged an update on the day. Then, she asked about me. I told her that I was dealing antiques down in the Village. I said that Hobie was my partner. She was pleased because she held an interest in old things too, which I from when I'd arrived in a few old pieces that decorated the place.

Mrs. Barbour lamented that none of her children had gotten her interest or eye for appreciating the arts. She remembered how I used to study her paintings. I cleared my throat with the intention of leaving soon. I said how wonderful it was to see them both when they asked me to stay for dinner. I couldn't, but was glad I had gotten to visit. Mrs. Barbour insisted that come back another day for dinner. I agreed and kissed her cheek good-bye.

4

Platt walked me out and awkwardly gave me a fist bump handshake. I told him it was nice to run into him and to give me a call. He then mentioned that he had been hanging out with my old friend, Tom Cable. I was surprised because I hadn't talked to him in so many years. Platt said that he had been confused as to why someone like me, who hung out with Cable, would hang out with his brother. He figured that since Cable had a reputation, I must have been like him. I wasn't.

I actually didn't know what he was talking about and figured that Cable probably had gone down a different path after I left. Platt said maybe that was true. Then, he said how his mother had thought I was so wonderful, but he hadn't bought it since I was friends with Tom. He had told Toddy and Kitsey to lock their rooms when I moved in because of this. It sort of made sense, considering the way they behaved around me back then. It didn't seem he had a real purpose in telling me about Tom, and then said he'd let his brother and sister know about catching up with me.

5

I needed to clear my head, so I walked towards the Village. The news about Andy left me disoriented. I had meant so many times over the years to call him, but different reasons had come up. I had run into a few old schoolmates, who kept me up on what he was doing.

In fact, it surprised me that I hadn't heard about his death sooner, but I had some problems with the shop lately and was distracted. The shop was doing well financially. Hobie had insisted on making me a partner as he credited me with the return of success with the shop. My main concern was that if we became partners, it would become clear that my success was partially attributed to the fact that I had taken to intentionally selling fakes to clients for the real prices. In fact, a client had discovered the truth and caused a bit of a fuss. I offered the money back at a loss. Yet, this particular client wasn't giving in.

Since Hobie's work was so good, I would convince buyers that the restored or altered pieces were the originals.

With the low light of the shop, the buyer wouldn't be able to notice the difference until they got it home. If someone realized and called, I would offer to buy it back at 10% more than it was sold. This made me look like a good guy who stood by his integrity and genuine remorse at knowing that what I had thought was an original was not.

Most of the time, clients accepted I hadn't meant to cheat them and kept the pieces. In some cases, they did return the pieces to me. In these instances, I would get the pieces to be proven or acquire a provenance that showed a paper trail that the piece was an original, since it had been sold as such. When I got the piece back, I could mark up the price again for resale and I had more proof that what I said about the piece was true.

I usually kept this kind of activity to the celebrities or socialites. With the regular dealers, I would stay true. A recent client named Lucius Reeve wasn't cooperating as others had. He wasn't accepting anything I had to offer, including the buyback option. I met him for lunch and left him a check to take care of the matter, but he hadn't yet cashed it. This was what I'd been checking on at the bank when I ran into Platt. The real concern was that Reeve was trying to drag Hobie into things, claiming that my insistence that Hobie knew nothing about the mistake was a cover up for Hobie.

When I went back to the storage unit that Grisha had first taken me to and looked through all that was there, I was amazed to find pieces that looked like originals. Hobie said none of them were real, but he had such a talent that he could take pieces which were in poor shape and make them almost new. For Hobie, it never occurred to him to sell his refurbished and remodeled pieces as originals. Now, I had free reign over the store.

Reeve said he found it too convenient that Hobie left all the business dealings to me. I wasn't comfortable with his line of questioning. I knew that Hobie wouldn't be happy to find out what I was doing. I learned a few tricks for selling items less than perfect. For example, if someone wanted to look at the piece in more detail, I made sure that area around was dirty to discourage them looking under the piece to reveal flaws. Some people liked the hunt of finding unique items, so I would bury important pieces to be 'found'. Once a piece was discovered or decided upon, I might play hard to get to raise the value of the item in the potential buyer's mind.

There was very little worry about anything going wrong at the time of sale. Hobie was usually in his workshop, but occasionally he would pop up. His friend, Mrs. DeFrees might appear, at which point I would end the closing of the sale. The news about Andy mixed with my concerns over this Lucius Reeve and led me to the Pond in the Park where Andy and I used to wait for my mother after elementary school, the Rendezvous Point.

Lately, I used the place to meet Jerome, a bike messenger who sold me drugs. After taking Xandra's stash of pills, I developed a habit over the years of mixing them. I had a set schedule of one day on and one day off, but the off days were becoming less frequent. I had managed to complete college, but had been so altered by my time in Vegas that my future in academics was limited. I wasn't motivated to work very hard. It took me six years to finish my undergraduate work, instead of the typical four.

My counselor didn't recommend that I pursue a master's degree since I wouldn't be eligible for scholarships. I didn't mind. I already knew that I wanted to work as an antique dealer. I had started working in the shop upstairs since I was 17. Grisha's words of caution about Hobie's financial situation were becoming more obvious around then. I noticed more notices due for payment, yet Hobie never opened the shop for more than a half hour. Most of the time, I would come back from school to see the "Closed" sign on the door and people would be peering in. If Hobie did keep the shop open, he would leave it unattended so people would come in and steal things.

One of the guys, Mike, who worked with Grisha in moving the furniture sometimes covered the store and would do what he could to make sure no one was taking advantage of Hobie's lack of concern for business. I started to study after school with my books in the shop while Hobie continued working downstairs. Over the years since Welty's death, the shop had become a target for regular theft and shoplifting. As I worked to change that reputation, I also learned the art of fluid pricing. Some customers had no idea about the value of an item and would pay more than it was worth. Others would come in having a good sense of an item's value, so I would adjust the pricing to their knowledge. I started to remove all price tags so customers would have to ask me for a price and I could adjust according to the type of buyer they appeared to be.

Another trick was that about a quarter of the prices in the store should be kept low for people who were looking for a bargain. It also allowed some freedom to further mark up the prices for items that truly deserved a higher tag. This was how I started in rebuilding the business of Hobart and Blackwell. I enjoyed the game of business as well as helping money to return Hobie.

While Hobie was talented at finding flaws in furniture and figuring out how to fix them, I found I was good at obfuscation and mystery in talking with people. It was part of the game to figure out what kind of purchase a person would be when they walked into the store. I started to read people well and changed the way I dressed to add to my image. With Lucius Reeve, I made a mistake.

I was in the Park at the Pond, looking at my mother's bench. An anonymous donor had inscribed *Everything of Possibility* on it. It was a bench my mother had used even before I was born. Nearby was the place that Andy and I had dropped her ashes.

6

Hobie was shocked at my appearance when I finally made it home. The Vogels were with him, all preparing to go out. Since I'd taken over the shop, the Vogels and I hadn't gotten along. I kept a watchful eye on them because of what Grisha told me. It wasn't clear to Hobie, but I tried to avoid them socially.

Hobie asked if I'd eaten and suggested that I join them for dinner. I declined and said I would eat in. Mr. Vogel offered his sympathies at my poor condition. Mrs. Vogel hinted that my state was due to Pippa's recent visit with her boyfriend. It's true that I hadn't been enthralled with her boyfriend or even the fact that she had one. Her recent visit was awkward and frustrating. I wanted to avoid her, but couldn't. She didn't help, being curious about everything I did and what I was listening to.

Her presence made me happy, but every time I tried to be alone with her, Everett – the boyfriend – would appear and they would go off on their own. I was unsettled the whole time. Once Hobie and the Vogels left, I realized that Mrs. Vogel hit closer to home than I'd expected. I'd become a little obsessive over Pippa. I spent most days thinking about her, wondering what she was doing.

Most people saw her differently. She had a slight limp and bright red hair that was shocking for most. I found her beautiful. I never told her so. For me, she was the missing piece of my mother. I wasn't impressed by Everett who seemed to enjoying using her money, left by Uncle Welty. I wondered if I could pay him to leave her alone. I knew that no one could care about her the way I did.

My fantasies never turned into anything and I loved her in secret. Twice, I tried kissing her, but she didn't return the affection and I was embarrassed. I apologized and she said it was ok. I could do no more without encouragement. Still, I couldn't change my feelings for her. To clear my head, I took one of the Oxycontins that I kept in an old tobacco tin on the dresser and felt good.

7

It was stormy on the night I went to the Barbours' for dinner. By the time I arrived, I was a wet mess. I didn't recognize Toddy at first. When he saw me, he gave me a wet hug and invited me in. Todd had grown up and was studying at Georgetown. He told me I'd influenced him to get into political science and work to help disadvantaged young people like I had been. I was impressed.

As Todd was talking about his interests, I heard heels coming down the hall. Kitsey came up and hugged me too, despite my drenched state. I was amazed at how beautiful she'd grown. They both left me speechless. I hadn't seen them since they were seven or eight.

Platt was there, too. Kitsey asked him where their mother wanted everyone. He said back in her quarter. As they were finishing getting ready, Kitsey grabbed me to go get a drink. She said she hoped they would be eating in the dining room or even the kitchen. She asked what I wanted and I chose the Stolichnaya vodka, which surprised her as her father was the only one who drank it.

She shared that she was afraid I wouldn't come. I said the weather wasn't that bad, but she meant that she thought that I hated them. This surprised me. She recalled that they had been difficult when I lived there, but it was so long ago. We had a drink and went in to see her mother. I recalled the way that Mr. Barbour had put his hand on a lady's elbow to accompany them into a room, so I did the same to Kitsey.

8

It was a mixed night of reminiscing and adjusting to the new ways of Mrs. Barbour. Who would have ever thought that Mrs. Barbour would be eating potpies on a folded table in her room? Everyone was happy to see me, even Etta, the cook, who waited for me to stop in the kitchen to give me a hug. Todd was the central figure, guiding the conversation throughout the evening. Before, Mrs. Barbour hadn't really wanted to talk about Andy, but with me she did so and mentioned the furniture pieces that had history in her house.

I didn't talk much to Kitsey but I noticed that she was watching me. Platt pulled me aside and mentioned that Kitsey was on antidepressants. It seemed understandable, given the circumstances. She had been the closest to Andy. I didn't remember that. Platt further revealed that she'd left Wellesley and would take some classes closer to home since it was difficult for her to be so near where the accident had happened. It was possible that she blamed herself, as she'd been the one to encourage Andy to go up to visit Mr. Barbour, instead of her.

I told Platt that she shouldn't take it so hard and shouldn't blame herself. The irony is that if she had been the one on the boat, they probably would have been fine. It was Andy's lack of interest in sailing that probably contributed to the situation. In any case, Kitsey was in a fragile state. Platt suggested that I ask her out to dinner, saying it would make Mrs. Barbour happy.

9

It was after 11 by the time I left the Barbours'. The rain had stopped. I was left thinking about how strange it still was to think that Andy was gone. He'd been the kindest to me when I needed it the most. I determined that the least I could do was to be extra kind to Andy's mother and sister in return for his kindness toward me.

10

Even though I'd claimed a controlled habit, I still had a habit. I was still always on edge as a leftover from the explosion. Once I started taking the painkillers, I worked my way up to stronger ones. Now, only the Oxy did the trick. My dealers told me I was spending a fortune on the pills and that I could get the same effect for cheaper if I switched to heroin. I only did heroin though if someone offered it to me. I enjoyed it, but I never bought it because I knew that if I did, I would never stop. I felt that with the pills, I could still control the habit.

It's generally believed that you can't function on opiates, but when you have post-traumatic stress disorder, it's almost necessary to take opiates to survive. Alcohol took away normal functions, but it was possible to function on the pills. I had no girlfriend or non-drug friends, I worked long days and stayed fairly serene. I had the image of being balanced and put together. I figured out how to survive in the game to maintain the business, which supported my drug habit.

There were a few times that I had slipped up or Hobie would notice that I was off, but I tried to hide it the best I could. When things seemed to be getting out of hand, I would do less or stop altogether. Once I stopped for six weeks. I convinced myself that people who were addicted couldn't do that. In the past three years I hadn't been clean more than three days in a row. I came up with a quitting plan. I would taper myself off over a seven-day period. I had all the things that I needed to help me with the process. The hardest part was the anticipation that after 36 hours, the worse part of withdrawals would hit.

The night I returned from the Barbours', I took a long-acting morphine tablet, which I did whenever I came up feeling guilty. I prepared a last combination of hits and took up the tin that had all I'd bought from Jerome. Rather than flush it all, I decided to take it to my storage locker. I hadn't been there more than three times in seven years. Mostly it was to make the yearly payment, which I now did for two years. Inside the locker, I saw that nothing had changed. There was an odor from the stale tape.

I had an urge to open and see the painting but I knew it would take time to unwrap it and more to wrap it back up. Still, I had such a strong urge. If I hadn't known there were security cameras watching me, I might have taken the painting back out with me. Instead, I left the tin in the bag and closed the locker back up.

11

I thought I had a pretty good control over my habit but the withdrawals hit me harder and faster than I expected. I told Hobie that I had a cold and would be fine. Since my stomach was where the problem was, Hobie declared that I had the flu and stocked up on the necessary remedies, suggesting I visit a doctor. He said I shouldn't be down in the workshop if I felt so bad, but the work was the only thing that took my mind off the misery. I tried to work through it while Popchyk, who had started to age, watched me anxiously. The physical effects were manageable, but the mental struggle was much more than I thought I could handle. The way I felt was far worse than depression. This was deep and dark despair, burdened with hopelessness. I was living a nightmare, day and night, as my dreams were filled with the same sense of misery.

Around the eighth day, I started to make my way back up the hill and managed to eat something, which gave Hobie some relief. He suggested that I take Popchyk out for some sun and fresh air, but I only intended to go to the safety of the quiet and dark shop. Hobie said I'd had a few calls. One call was from Daisy Horsley, the code name for a woman I'd been seeing off and on. Then, a woman called with an offer on a cherry wood high-chest which Hobie accepted while I was out of commission. Platt had called. Lucius Reeve had called twice.

12

I wasn't yet ready to deal with Lucius Reeve and wasn't that into speaking with Platt, but thankfully Kitsey was the one who answered the phone. She said they were going to have another dinner for me. I was surprised, but seeing me had lifted Mrs. Barbour's spirits, so they were hoping I would return soon.

She put Platt on the line. He called me brother. That was weird. I heard that Kitsey left the room and he became direct in his purpose. Platt wanted me to try to sell some of the furniture in the house. He didn't want to involve Mrs. Barbour. I didn't know why he wanted to sell anything. There was something he wasn't saying.

I said it was a complicated process and I would have to see each item before I could do or say anything about selling. Platt suggested that he could send me photos and I said that wouldn't work. I explained that I didn't deal with coins or ceramics as they were some of the items he mentioned wanting to sell. Then, I had an idea and a suggestion for him, if he just needed a bit of cash right away. He was interested.

I explained that I needed to get a provenance established for a piece, the one I'd sold to Lucius Reeve, and that if I could get a bill of sale proving I'd bought it from another collector, then maybe this guy would leave me alone. Platt offered that his mother would do just about anything for me, but I explained that I needed this to be in the strictest of confidence, which he quickly understood. We came up with the plan that Platt would be the collector I mentioned. If the guy phoned, then Platt would explain that he'd sold it because it was just sitting up at their place in Maine. The other details he had down. We agreed that if he could help me with this, then I would I would give him 10% of the price of the piece, which was $7,000. Platt was pleased with the arrangement.

13

I felt better about the entire situation after talking with Platt. I was a bit disturbed by Platt's desire to sell Mrs. Barbour's things without her knowledge as she had quite a few important pieces. There was no doubt that Platt was in some kind of situation. I remembered that something had happened all those years ago when Platt was expelled from Groton. We never knew what he did, but whatever it was may have led him to his current troubles. Feeling more confident, I called Lucius Reeve. I asked him what he wanted and he said that we should meet. Since we'd met on his turf before, I chose the place this time.

14

I picked a place that wasn't in a regular neighborhood, but was modern enough to have a crowd that Lucius Reeve wasn't comfortable with. I was waiting when he arrived. He didn't approve of my choice of seating, right in the middle of the room. The place was busy, though, and he gave in, taking his seat. We ordered food, which Lucius didn't appear to like. I had a carbon of the fake bill of sale in my picket, but wouldn't produce it unless I needed to.

As Lucius began to eat, he looked at me and said, "I know about the museum."

I was surprised. "Know what?"

He told me that I should know exactly what he was talking about. I feigned ignorance instead focusing on it as a bad time when my mother died and that I didn't particularly want to discuss the topic with him. Lucius already knew that and also that Welton Blackwell had died that day. What was more important was that somehow he found out that Hobie had told the story of how I came to his place with Welty's ring. I said I didn't know what his point was, but he refused to believe me.

"You have something I want. That a lot of people want, actually," he said.

I stopped midway to my mouth and had an urge to just get up and walk out.

When Reeve thought he'd caught me, I recovered with a reiteration that I had no idea what he was getting at. I explained my confusion that we were meant to be talking about the chest-on-chest piece that was of concern. Reeve pushed the point that he had put together the fact that I'd been in the same room as Welton Blackwell and his niece in Gallery 32. Also, missing from Gallery 32, was something important, which he merely hinted at.

I felt the blood drain from me. He taunted my naiveté in thinking that no one would figure it out. Plus, there was the seeming coincidence that I then came under the care of Hobie. I continued with my ignorance, which started to annoy him. He said the painting was beautiful and unique. He'd seen it before in the Mauritshius. He talked about it as if he knew a lot about the painting. He even knew the story about it being found in some storeroom in the 1890s.

Having learned from my father the technique of denying everything no matter what, I continued that line with Lucius. He kept on with his imagined story and I kept on being confused about what he was trying to say. He finally said I could keep denying, but that he thought I was a fool to trust anyone with it. This part was a real surprise to me as I absolutely had no idea what he was talking about. I was starting to get annoyed.

He said that what he was offering was to buy the painting from me. He suggested that half a million would be appropriate. He claimed to be able to make a phone call and end the entire enterprise. I again said that I had no idea what he was talking about.

He seemed convinced that I was working with a group of people and that the best interest for me and the painting was to sell it to him. He passed a copy of an Internet article talking about how it was believed that a master painting – *The Goldfinch* – had been lost in a raid in South Florida where stolen artworks were found. The authorities believed the painting had gone underground after the raid in South Florida and they had no idea if or when it would be seen again.

They believed the painting had already left the States for Hamburg, where it could be auctioned for many millions. I put down the paper and saw that Reeve was watching me carefully. As I looked at him, I started to laugh. I told him he must be delusional or something. I apologized for laughing, but told him it was the most absurd thing I had ever heard. Reeve still refused to accept what I was saying. He said that he was offering me a way out. I asked, "A way out of what?"

He said he was ready to phone the man in the art-crimes division and tell him that he knew Hobie and me were part of the grand scheme. At that, I pushed away from the table and told him to go, right away. As I left, I told him to get in touch should he want to solve the initial matter between us.

15

Once I was three or four blocks away, I began to shake so violently that I had to sit on a bench and control my breathing. I thought of trying to find Jerome for a quick fix. He only sold in large amounts, but I knew he would be able to give me something small. The tinnitus in my ears was oppressive in my head. It occurred to me that the initial problem with Reeve was so small compared to this new revelation. I worried about Hobie and knew that I would have to tell him the truth, at least about selling fakes.

The article confused me because they had no real proof that I had a painting. However, it did seem that a fake copy was floating around and this incident with the chest supported the idea that Hobie and I were somehow involved in selling a fake version of *The Goldfinch*. I should have done something with the painting long ago. If I got caught I would deserve whatever punishment was handed down. I just wanted to bury the painting somewhere deep and out of my mind.

16

When I made it back home, I went to talk to Hobie. I needed to come clean about the selling of the fakes as originals, at least. I started out that I was in a bit of a jam. Hobie asked how he could help. I had to reveal that I had inadvertently included him in the jam, which still didn't get his attention enough to stop his work. He finally paused and asked what I was trying to say.

I admitted to making a stupid mistake and told him a version of what I'd done, starting with the current incident with Lucius Reeve. Once I started telling him, I couldn't stop and Hobie stopped just listening to me. He told me to stop explaining, that he understood what I was getting at. I apologized and he hesitated before responding. Hobie was very calm. He said it was done and that all I could do was try to fix it. The more he tried to pass it off as something that would work out, the more I felt upset by his calmness. Then, I revealed that I'd been doing this kind of thing for a while with some of the pieces that were out in storage. He was still calm and asked how I was going to deal with these things.

It was unnerving how calm he was, so I explained that I would take full responsibility. He was processing the whole situation. The pieces were out there and so far no one had been in contact about the deception. He asked how long I'd been doing it. I told him two years instead of the actual five or more.

He was shocked, but said he was glad I told him the truth. He felt that I should contact the clients and tell them the truth. If they wanted us to buy back the pieces, then we would. The only problem was that we didn't have that much money. I also hadn't kept a close client list. The more truth I revealed, I could see it slowly cracking away at Hobie's calm. He told me how this calls everything that he does in to question. His reputation was on the line. I knew that, but never really thought it would become an issue.

Hobie thought I had more to say, but I just apologized. He admitted to his own fault in the situation by not paying more attention to where the money was coming from and that in some ways, people would think I was a genius for what I'd done. He was most concerned by our reputation, as that would make or break someone in the profession. Hobie said it was important that I take care of this situation now or it was going to come back to get us both later. Then there was silence, with nothing more to say. Hobie didn't want to talk about it, again. I could tell that he wanted to be left alone. I didn't know what to do.

17

Originally, I intended to give Hobie this easy news before dropping the big news. After our conversation, though, I knew that I couldn't involve him at all in the painting. I wished there was at least someone I could share the burden with. Over the years, there had been mention here and there about the painting, but no clear ideas of what happened, so most had determined that it must have gotten thrown into the fire when the explosion hit, since it was so close to the source.

The official stories on me said that I was nowhere near the room with *The Goldfinch* at the time of the explosion. Most stories assumed that I'd been near my mother, leaving me safe from inquiry. Hobie talked enough to different people about Welty's death and how I'd come to have his ring. Someone was bound figure it out eventually. I knew, but hoped that no one would.

I sat on my bed feeling shaky and bad, desperately wanting a pill. I got up to get a drink and noticed a figure standing out on the street, watching the store. As I watched him, I turned the lamp off and the man moved out of the streetlight. He stayed a bit longer and finally walked away. I saw that he was calling someone as he left. Due to my usual paranoid state, I figured I must have been imagining the man, that he wasn't really watching the place.

I went to get a drink and took out my phone. I was naturally going to call Jerome, but hung up and called the Barbours. Etta answered the phone and asked if I wanted to speak to Katherine, as everyone except her family and close friends knew her. I asked if she was there, but Etta said she was coming later for dinner and had been waiting for my call. I left a message and hung up after Etta told me to come visit again soon.

I began to think about Reeve again. He had shown his hand too soon by not focusing on the furniture more. Why was he going after me for the painting? He could have waited until I led him to it instead of being so direct. I was still safe as long as no one knew where the painting was. As long as I didn't go near the storage unit, there was no way to make the connection.

Chapter Ten: Secrets Revealed

1

It was shortly before Christmas and I was at lunch with Kitsey. I gave her my mother's emerald earrings. She exclaimed that they were beautiful, but hesitated. She said that her complexion wasn't made for the stone, but she promised to wear them for the wedding. She could tell I was annoyed, though I denied it. I was tired. We'd spent the morning at Tiffany's and most of our time these days was spent picking out stuff for the wedding or trying to find a place to live. I was being picky about where we'd live as it had to be just right, without any sense that anything negative ever happened there before.

We put up with each other's oddities throughout the process, but doing the wedding registry was not my idea of fun, especially so close to the holidays. It was hard for me to pretend to like anything, even though Kitsey did her best to include me in the decisions of china patterns. None of it mattered. We were back to the earrings. She knew they had been my mother's so she said she would wear them. I said it didn't matter.

2

Our relationship had happened quickly. Within two months, we were inseparable, seeing each other every day for walks and dinner. We talked about the old times and never had difficulty keeping the conversation going. I had decided to move on with my life, after spending years in love with Pippa. She never gave me any encouragement to pursue her and I realized that it wasn't healthy to continue on this way. We saw each other twice a year and texted sporadically. I accepted that we were just friends.

The decision to let go of my yearning was a conscious one that took everything I could to do it. Having done it, I was free to enjoy being with Kitsey. She stayed in the city for the first time in her life and we had fun together. She begged me to hang out with her when she couldn't handle being stuck at home with her mother anymore. We went to East Hampton and stayed in her friend's house. On the weekdays, we would meet after I finished work and enjoy a drink and dinner.

It was Kitsey who asked me to get married. It was subtle, but I knew what she was asking and I agreed. The date wasn't set, but we were taking care of everything else, constantly. It felt like the wedding plans were going wild, but I tried to be pleasant about it. Mrs. Barbour was happy when we announced that we wanted to get married. I treasured that moment, to have her on one side, beaming, and Kitsey on the other, equally pleased because of me. The realization that I could make anyone happy was soothing for the soul. Up to then, I'd kept myself so closed off and unhappy that this new summer passed blissfully. Kitsey became my new obsession.

I knew I was lucky to be marrying Kitsey. Yet, sometime around October, the darkness started to return. I despised being around people, I lost the ability to concentrate or socialize and it seemed that everything was again hopeless. I was taking anti-depressants that didn't seem to work. I just got headaches and darker thoughts. I would have moments of relief only to have the darkness flood back in. I couldn't explain why.

Kitsey and I were always in the company of others. There was always some event to attend and all of that made me tired. Add on the stress of socializing, the wedding plans and work, it was taking a toll. Despite the dark points, I did feel sure about my future. I felt that this was the right thing for me and it made me happy to bring joy to Mrs. Barbour and to Kitsey. I could see changes to Mrs. Barbour since our engagement and it was a nice feeling to know I contributed to her brighter moods. She told me that she always thought of me as one of her own. I was touched and didn't know what to say, but I kept the memory of learning this truth as a precious item.

Telling Pippa about Kitsey was bittersweet. I could tell she was surprised, but she said she was happy for me. I gushed too much about Kitsey, but it wasn't a lie when I said I'd loved Kitsey since I was little. There was actually something very enticing about this truth. We'd been very different as kids, yet now we were being naughty in her childhood bedroom. Every day, I reminded myself of how lucky I was. Kitsey was amazing in all areas. Even Hobie really liked her.

One thing strange about Kitsey was her constraint or control over her emotional expressions. It seemed very concerning that she never showed any emotion about the death of Andy and her father. I'd never seen any reaction from her and thought maybe it would come out one day. We were still having lunch when Kitsey suggested going to Barney's. I said that I had to get to back downtown to meet a client. She asked if I was going to make it out later and begged that I come for cocktails. I promised to try and reminded her of the earrings. She dropped them into her bag like they were nothing.

3

I felt down as we walked out. There was no reason for me to feel this way or to be bitter towards Kitsey for her ability to move on so easily. Nothing major had come from

Reeve since our last lunch visit. No one had called the shop to complain about forged pieces. Overall, everything was going just fine. I felt like it would all hit eventually, and once the first person stepped up, it would be bad.

I worried that this would come out before we got married. Then, what would I do? Not only would Hobie be involved, but now, so would Kitsey and her mother. If it happened after we were married, we could work things out. Still, the Barbours' financial situation wasn't as good as it had been and everyone was worried about money coming in. When we got engaged, Platt seemed thrilled, since he knew I would be able to make money.

More disturbing than all of this was Lucius Reeve. He sent me letters, repeating his offer and letting me know that he hadn't forgotten the situation. I tried to forget about him, but a couple of things happened, which caused me worry more. First, Hobie received a letter directly from Reeve. I told Hobie that this was the guy from the original incident and to just throw away his letter. I tried to explain Reeve's hair brain idea that we were running some sort of illegitimate business and how he wanted in on it. That was why he hadn't cashed the check I'd written. Hobie was perturbed by this suggestion.

Hobie said he was going to keep Lucius' card, as there was more than enough for us to call the police on him, if necessary. Hobie wasn't upset about the piece as much as he was annoyed that there might be anything illegal. It was silly to worry too much about Reeve, as there was still nothing to prove that I had the painting. Yet, it also made me wish I could look at the painting. When we looked at apartments, I imagined where I could hide it.

Worry still gripped me over its safety and the environmental controls for the lockers. No matter how much I wanted to move it or see it, I knew that with Reeve on my tail, there was no way. Soon, the payment would be due and I wouldn't be able to go, myself. I figured Grisha or one of the guys would go for me without asking.

Then, the second thing happened. Grisha needed to talk to me. He asked me if I was being investigated or followed for some reason. I said I didn't think so. He didn't seem convinced, but announced that he and Mike had noticed people watching the shop. He was concerned, as his cousin wanted him to help out, but he wouldn't do if it meant leading the police to him. I said that I had no idea what was going on. He said it had been four or five times that he'd seen someone hanging around.

According to Mike, this had been going on for more than a month. The others, like Grisha, had no idea. I asked Grisha to let me know the next time he sees anyone doing that. He agreed and said that the day before, someone new had come in the shop and asked for me. He didn't leave a name. I asked that they let me know if they see anyone again. I told him I didn't think he had anything to worry about, but he wasn't convinced.

4

I had lied to Kitsey. There was no client to meet. I just needed a break. She had gone back to Tiffany's and I went to take the 6 train. Seeing all the people at the station stopped me, so I paused and stared at the Subway Inn. I recalled a time that we'd all gone shopping and my father had just disappeared. Somehow, my mom knew to find him at a nearby bar where he'd had a couple of shots.

I decided to start walking. I felt like the walking dead as I made my way through the crowded streets, seeing all the Christmas decorations. Since I hadn't gone into a bar, I thought I would try a movie. I figured a mostly empty movie theater would give me some comfort. By the time I got to the cinema, the movies worth seeing had either already started or weren't to start for a while.

I made it to Union Square and thought to call Jerome. I hadn't done any drugs in months and I didn't even know if he would have anything good on him, but I thought it would be a nice way to spend an evening. The thought of the crazy big wedding that was going to happen was nearly enough to make me go nuts, but I planned to take a few Xanax and I would get through.

I wasn't fully prepared for the social life I was facing with trying to chat with couples where the men sat and talked about their sailing clubs or the women discussed being pregnant or both shared the joys of parenting. I wasn't even sure I would like my own child. After all, my father and his father hadn't liked their children. A night in pharmaceutical bliss sounded perfect. Since I wasn't taking pills, I had started drinking more, but that wasn't as good for me. I didn't really relax on booze.

It had been some time since I had called Jerome and the number I dialed went straight to voice mail. It didn't sound like his message even. I wondered if he'd disappeared, as people like him were wont to do when necessary. My options were thinning out and I kept wandering, not knowing what to do. At some point, I recalled that Jerome told me about a bar with a red awning in St. Mark's. There was a bartender there who dealt from behind the counter. Her name was Katrina, but I didn't know where the bar was.

I went to a few bars and asked for her, but no one knew her. I found a bar with a black awning but red letters and asked for Katrina. The guy at the bar stopped and looked at me. I said I was a friend of Jerome's. The guy wasn't too friendly after that, asking me more questions that I didn't have answers to, so I quickly made my way out of the bar. I had gone a bit down the street when I heard "Potter!" shouted out behind me.

I hadn't heard that name in years. I turned in disbelief, and there before me was Boris. He laughed and threw his arms around me. I was stunned. He said he'd stopped by my shop the other day. That must have been whom Mike had met. Boris thought I was down there looking for him, but I said no. This was just chance. He told me I looked terrible and we joked around like old times. I asked why he hadn't left a number at the shop. He thought maybe I was angry with him or something, but I assured him that wasn't the case. Then, there was a woman with us, calling me Potter.

Her name was Myriam, and I introduced myself as Theo. She knew, but Boris only called me Potter. There was something between them, but I didn't know what. Boris asked if I was going to be around the neighborhood. I said I could stick around. Myriam gave me the location of a bar four or five blocks away and said he would meet me there in about an hour.

5

It was almost three hours later when I started thinking I should just go home. It was a shock to see Boris again. I'd Googled him before to see if anything would come up on him, but there was no information about him at all. I had three vodkas and was getting hungry and moody as time went on. I thought he'd just blown me off after all these years. Just as I was making up my mind to go, he slid into the booth next to me. He apologized lightly, saying he had something to do and thought that Myriam had explained. I said that she hadn't.

He intimated that his work wasn't so regular. He told me not to be mad as he'd come as fast as he could. He'd grown up nicely and had changed. He said he married a Swede and I thought he meant Myriam. He quickly clarified that his wife and kids were still in Sweden. They looked beautiful and far too perfect.

I thought maybe they were divorced, but Boris explained that his wife and kids were mostly in Stockholm, as she liked to be near the mountains. She was an Olympic qualified ski champion. I asked who Myriam was as Boris dug into some food that had magically appeared, as it was a bar with no food. Boris said she worked for him.

He said he lived all over the place and that his official business was called a housecleaning agency. I told him I thought he'd gone back to Russia since I hadn't heard from him ever again. Boris explained that it was messed up time after I left. He'd taken to regularly buying and selling drugs. The school kids had gone crazy getting stuff from him and he was making a lot of money.

He'd ended up staying with Xandra for a while because his dad had gone to Australia and he and Kotku were on the rocks again. He had had a softer feeling for Xandra and said that they hooked up, though I didn't care for the details. It turned out that Boris had gone to work for Bobo Silver after he'd come around to make sure that Xandra didn't know anything about my father's debts. Boris helped Xandra get back on her feet with his drug money from school.

Boris asked about me after that. He heard that things were going well, but noticed that I wasn't happy and offered me a job working with him. I laughed. He was serious and said I could make twice what I was now, but I said I like my job. I was unhappy for other reasons. He surmised that if it wasn't my job, then it had to be money problems or a girl. Suddenly, I had a great idea. I wanted him to come with me, but he was suspicious. If I hadn't had so much to drink, I would have been angry at his hesitation. It was like when I wanted to leave Vegas. He asked what the surprise was and I told him to come with me and he'd find out. After much cajoling, he finally agreed, but only as long as we went with his driver.

6

Boris was acting so paranoid that it almost made me laugh. I told him to come in, but he still didn't want to. He finally stepped inside and Hobie called out. He came to the hallway, dressed for dinner. Mrs. DeFrees was there. I went to introduce Boris to them when he yelled out "Popchyk!" Popchyk paused upon hearing his name and then went flying and yapping to Boris. He fell to his knees, laughing. Their reunion left me and Hobie watching, amused. Mrs. DeFrees seemed less so, having smelled the vodka on Boris and watching them catch up. Hobie had figured out who the guest was by this point.

7

Since we were rather drunk and boisterous, I felt like we were upsetting Mrs. DeFrees, so we didn't stay long at the house. Instead, we took Popchyk and headed to Boris' car. His driver, Gyuri, who hadn't spoken a word of English to me on the way there, suddenly seemed to be fluent in it as we drove down the West Side Highway with Boris fawning all over Popchyk. Boris seemed so pleased that we'd found each other again and was regaling Gyuri with how fortunate we were. Gyuri agreed, comparing us to his brother, Vadim. He told us the story of him and Vadim while he drove, throwing us around in the back seat.

For some reason, Gyuri thought my name was Fyodor and asked me questions about God. Boris corrected him pointing out that God had not been overly kind to me. Boris asked Gyuri for a favor, to watch the dog while we went inside the club. We were somewhere in Queens. It was a place where Boris was well known. He was walking around, introducing me to everyone as his brother. We eventually made it to the back of the place and sat. Myriam appeared from nowhere and she and Boris disappeared, leaving me alone with a bunch of stoned and drunk Russians. Thanks to Boris, I was in good hands. A strange woman named Zhanna approached me. She tried to engage me in conversation until Boris returned and made her disappear. He said he had never seen her before, but they seemed friendly enough. After that, Boris said we could go if I wanted and that Gyuri was waiting outside.

8

It was late, but we drove around for hours with Popychyk sleeping happily on Boris' lap. Gyuri would join our conversation now and then. Boris recalled how my father had taught him the importance of dressing right. I could see that Boris had taken the lessons to heart.

As he was rolling up his sleeves, I noticed he had a tattoo of the Star of David. I also saw that he had a lot of needle marks, but I didn't mention those. It seemed that Boris wanted to make a good impression on Bobo Silver to convince him to give him a job. He had gotten the tattoo to impress him. In the end, Mr. Silver hadn't bought it, but hired him anyway. I was surprised that Boris would work for someone who wanted to kill my dad, but Boris said that wasn't the case. He just wanted to scare him. For a year, Boris worked for Bobo Silver. His work was mostly being a messenger boy, walking his dogs and things like that. Mr. Silver was kind to him and Boris had a fondness for him. Boris had another tattoo of a woman's name , Katya, who he claimed was the love of his life. He said she was really amazing, but that no one should get tattoos of a person's name, because then you lose the person.

9

It was 6:30am and no chance of sleeping. I hadn't done any cocaine for a while and I was wired out. I told Boris how I'd taken conversational Russian for a year in college because of him. I never got good enough to read *Eugene Onegin* in its original. I admitted that I'd thought of him a lot throughout my college years, remembering our times in Vegas. Boris was unimpressed with my schooling, saying I should have gone with him to Russia if I wanted to learn Russian. I finally asked what exactly he did. He said, "This and that, just enough to get by."

He noticed my spirits had lifted. When he'd first seen me, I'd been pretty low. I said it was a rough day. Boris asked if we were partners, meaning intimate since he had always believed that Hobie was gay. I exclaimed, "NO.!" Then he asked if Mrs. DeFrees was his lady. I said, "Yes," but I didn't know the details of their relationship. She was married, but they didn't live together even though they still did many things together. I had never really seen her husband, though.

Boris went back to the subject of Hobie and asked if he'd taught me the trade. I said we were business partners and that I ran the sales side of things. Boris reiterated that he'd been serious about me going to work for him, but how was I supposed to respond to that. I guess Boris felt sort of guilty and felt like he wanted to give something back to me. He attributed all the good things in his life to me.

"What? I got you in the drug-dealing business? Wow, okay," I said. I wasn't sure if I wanted to take that as a compliment or not. Boris was confused. He wasn't talking about drug dealing. He said what he does is a great life. I tried to then suggest his business was an escort business. He didn't respond and went another direction by apologizing for what he did to me. I shrugged it off.

He kept pushing that he wanted to share his profits with me. I was direct with him, saying I didn't want to get involved in anything illegal, as I was doing my best to stay on top these days. Now that I had Kitsey in my life, I really needed to be on the even keel. He interrupted and said he could help me. I said that wasn't what I meant. I hinted at the fact that I'd done some things and wanted to try to fix them. That was what I was trying to do. Boris said that sometimes it's not possible to do that, but just try not to get caught. Then, he said something strange. "I've been trying to get it back for you."

"What?"

He said that it was why he'd gone to the store. He'd been worried that they caught up with me about the Miami stuff and that he'd been worried. It was a mistake for me to do more coke. I'd already done more than I should have. Boris was talking quickly, asking if I had thought about how to get it back. He said he couldn't use it anymore and that it wasn't exactly why he had come to see me. He really wanted to say he was sorry and to tell me not to worry about what was on the news. He was saying he didn't want me to hear it and thinking of how it would get back to me. He kept going and going.

I stared at him and said, "Boris, what are you talking about?"

"You know."

"No, I don't."

He didn't want to have to spell it out, but I didn't know at all what he was talking about. He said that if I had just waited one more day. Suddenly, things were colliding together and I could see Lucius Reeve sitting next to me.

No, it wasn't. No. Boris asked if I thought my dad had taken it. He'd hoped so. Then, he admitted it. He'd switched it. It was him.

"How? What?" I stared at him. He said he thought I knew that he had it hiding in his locker as a joke. He swore that he wasn't going to keep it, but I wouldn't stay just one more night so he could give it back to me. He was scared to tell me what he had done.

I was speechless. My heart was pounding uncontrollably. Boris looked deflated, thinking I wanted to kill him and was angry. I was still trying to comprehend what he was saying to me.

"What do you mean. you *switched* it?"

He apologized and said he knew it wasn't smart for us to get high together. He kept saying how bad he felt and started to get defensive, promising to make it up to me because he made a fortune from the painting. I asked him, then, what was in the package I had hiding in the storage locker. He was shocked that I'd never opened it up after all this time. I was dumbfounded.

Boris slammed the table and called me an idiot. How was it possible that after all these years I had not looked at it? I couldn't say anything. Boris shook me and confirmed that I really never opened it to look. It was Boris's turn to be shocked. How did I not know? I was beyond speechless. It hit him suddenly that I really had never known and the shock that I must be feeling.

"How did you even know I had it?"

Boris explained that I was blackout drunk, meaning that I did or said things that I didn't remember doing, like his father. I denied it, but he said my memory goes away when I'm drunk. He recalled some examples of times we were plastered and I had forgotten things that happened. He gave more examples and even tried to joke that I was the only guy who'd ever shared his bed.

I laughed, but somehow with anger. He tried to justify it, but got to the point. We'd been watching *Dr. No?* I stopped to listen, as I'd been about to get up to go. Boris knew I didn't remember watching the film because he would test me to see if I recalled anything. It was early in our friendship and I hadn't yet gotten used to drinking vodka. He kept asking if I remembered and since there were so many nights like that, I didn't.

Boris confessed that I used to get so upset, crying and telling him things how I thought it was my fault that my mother died or that I wished I had died. I was a big mess, then. According to Boris, I was pretty nuts. On the *Dr. No* night, I had seen a similar scene from the movie and decided to show Boris the painting. At the time, Boris hadn't believed anything I was saying, but once he set eyes on it, he knew that it was the real deal.

I said, "I don't believe you."

He continued with his story, but I refused to believe it. He rolled his eyes and brought up a picture on his phone. It was the backside of the painting. Most can reproduce the front of paintings, but the back was like the fingerprint of a painting."Believe me now?" he asked. I was thunderstruck. There was complete stillness.

Finally, without a word, I got my coat and went to leave. He tried to stop me. He told me not to be angry, that he really intended to pay me back. As he chased me out, I got into a cab and left him by a bank of trashcans.

10

I went straight to the storage locker, got the package I thought was the painting and was back in my room at Hobie's by 9:45am. I brought back everything from the locker. It took me 20 minutes of slowly unwrapping everything to eventually find a scribbled up Civics workbook. The contrast of the content of the book and how I felt was too much. It was Boris' schoolbook.

Hobie was out and I took some pills that didn't kick in. After trying to sleep, I gave up and cleaned up the room. I showered and sat down for some food and coffee and was in the shop by noon. It dawned on me then that Reeve could do whatever he wanted because he had nothing on me. I felt as if I was spinning, thinking back to all the years spent worrying about the painting *that wasn't even there.* I felt waves of relief and depression, simultaneously. I wasn't sure how to feel or what to do.

The painting was a piece of my identity. I'd believed that by having it hidden away, I held some kind of super power, by keeping the truth secret. Suddenly, this part of myself was taken from me. My entire adult life was based on a truth that wasn't true.

11

Hobie came in around 2:00 and was in high spirits, having done well at the auction house. He mentioned what a surprise it was to meet Boris. He asked if we had a good night. I couldn't respond. My head was killing me. Hobie compared his vision of Boris as one of the orphan boys in the Dickens' novel, *Oliver.* He mentioned how the Artful Dodger character in the novel had grown up to be quite successful, as it seemed that Boris had. Hobie was amazed at Popper's reaction, too.

At the sound of Popper's name, I paused. Then, Hobie let me know that Kitsey had called late and he'd told her that I'd run into Boris. Hobie paused trying to recall what Kitsey had asked him to tell me. He couldn't remember. When he said I needed to phone her, he remembered that we had dinner at 8 that night, but he didn't know where. I knew, and then Hobie continued on about Boris. He suggested we have Boris over one night if he's free. I didn't respond.

12

I'd left Popper behind, but how could I get him back while explaining why he was gone? None of the possible options were believable. My head was aching and I knew that Hobie would return in another hour or so, wondering where the dog had gone. There would be no denying the obvious once that happened. I paced from the window to my chair trying to figure out what to do. What was I going to tell Hobie?

I heard the shop bell ring. Popper was a bit damp, but he seemed fine. Boris said that he hadn't missed me at all and that they had a lovely day. I asked what they'd done. They had slept and Gyuri dropped them off. Boris had cleaned up and they went for a walk, but not too far because Popper was too old to go far. As he was telling me about his day with Popper, he abruptly apologized and promised to make things right again. There was a deafening silence between us.

He asked if I had fun last night and said that he had. He asked me to at least say something because he'd been feeling bad all day. He called me by my name, expressing his shame. All I could manage was, "Why ?" I kept my voice low, even though there was no way that Hobie would hear us, "Why the hell did you take it?"

He gave half reasons that I didn't buy and then admitted to plain and simply being a thief. I wanted to know what he wanted it for, but he didn't have an answer. It wasn't even about the money. He explained how he'd done it after finding it in my locker one day.

Boris said he wasn't denying the truth nor was he dishonest, but I said it wasn't true. He claimed he hadn't lied since I never asked him about it. If I had, he would have told me. I didn't accept that.

He said that at least he wasn't lying now. He thought I would have found out sooner and that I would have known it was him. He thought the painting was still in Europe, but earlier he'd mentioned deciding to deal with people he didn't know, causing a problem. Boris said he would explain everything after we'd both rested. He promised to make some calls and when he knew more, he would let me know. With a final comment about where I knicked myself shaving, we said goodbye. I watched him go, saw his steps lighten the further away he went and I was certain I would never see him again.

13

I was feeling so awful with my migraine and depressed state, I decided to close the shop. I was supposed to meet Kitsey at 7:45, before going to the Longstreets' for dinner. I arrived earlier because I wanted to talk to her privately and because I wanted to give something to Mrs. Barbour, a somewhat rare exhibition catalogue.

First, I went to see Mrs. Barbour who was up and walking around in her bedroom area. She seemed pleased with the gift. She said she'd seen the exhibition when she was in college in Boston. I felt happier than I would have thought possible just an hour before. Before, I was sick with everything and wondering how I'd survive. I'd even tried to call Kitsey to change plans, but she didn't respond to any of my calls or messages. She claimed there was something wrong with her phone, but when I offered to take get a new one, she had an excuse.

I'd taken a mild dose of opiates, which greatly lifted my mood. The Longstreets had been in the same class as Andy and I. Forrest Longstreet was awful to us and Mrs. Barbour recalled the boys who picked on us. She brought up Tom Cable, saying how badly he turned out. We bitterly reminisced about how awful that group of boys had been. We talked about how much Andy had been picked on by the others boys. Mrs. Barbour sighed.

As Mrs. Barbour kept looking through the book I'd brought for her, I glanced at the photos on the table beside us. We heard Platt coming and he seemed hesitant to say anything. Cautiously, he said Kitsey had been held up. That seemed to be some kind of code that only the family understood. I asked for clarification about where she was. They didn't answer and finally Mrs. Barbour said she thought Kitsey was out playing golf today.

That was surprising, since the weather was so bad. Platt jumped in saying that she was stuck in traffic and that the roads were a mess. She had already called ahead to the Longstreets, who would hold dinner. Mrs. Barbour suggested that Platt and I go out for a drink. It was decided as she smiled and thanked me for the book.

I paused, saying that if Kitsey had been playing golf, she would need to pop in to change and freshen up before going out again. Neither responded and I offered to stay and wait. Mrs. Barbour was quiet and I realized that she was probably tired, so I changed my mind and said a cocktail would be good. Just then, my phone chimed with a text from Kitsey. She said she was an hour late and would meet me at the Longstreets'.

14

It took me almost a week to recover from my night with Boris. I was extremely busy with work and going out with Kitsey each night. All week, I was looking forward to a night alone, when Kitsey was going out with girlfriends and Hobie was going out for dinner.

At closing time, I still had some things to do when Boris popped up and knocked on the door I'd just locked. It was still pouring rain and he was a bit hard to recognize. I finally let him in and he asked if I wanted to ride uptown with him. I said I was busy. He was hurt and said he thought I would want to go. I asked where and he said he was going to talk with some people about the painting, which I deduced more from his hesitation rather than his directness. He said I didn't have to come, but he thought that maybe I would want to. Popchyk came over to be properly greeted. The guy to be spoken with was someone Myriam knew and he'd taken losses in the deal, so she thought it would be a good idea to speak with him.

15

On the way uptown, with Gyuri driving, Boris explained Horst. His father made a lot of money, but Horst was a heavy junkie. He fell in love with a girl who took his money and ran. Horst's family disowned him after that and he was still heartbroken over the girl. Horst was involved in all of this because he had someone to set up meetings, although he never met the guy he set Boris up with.

Instead of getting everything he was promised in working with these guys, Boris only got half the amount he was promised, with the rest coming a week later. It was a fairly common practice, but then those guys got arrested and Boris didn't get the painting. Horst wants to find the painting, too. Boris was hoping he would have more information than he did the last time they spoke.

16

We were near the Barbours' place when we arrived at Horst's father's home. We were buzzed up and a blonde woman opened the door. She wordlessly let us in and left us alone in the salon. While we waited, I looked around at the artwork on the walls. I was about to inspect one of the paintings when a man appeared, looking a bit rough.

He seemed to know me and greeted me. He spoke to Boris, saying he was glad he'd come and that dinner was being made. Boris said we couldn't stay as he picked up a cat at our feet. Horst said to me, "You're a dealer, right?"

I confirmed that this was true. Another attractive woman came into the room, offering a bottle to Horst and one to me. Horst offered and Boris declined. He got down to business, wanting to know what he'd heard from Sascha, the guy who sets up his meets.

Ireland was the lead and it was good news, according to Horst. Boris said it didn't sound right and Horst agreed. Horst checked it out and so far it was holding. They were hoping for more news soon. It was clear that this place was used to create art, but I was uncomfortable. Boris asked why they would go to Ireland and what kind of collectors' market was there. He thought people tried to get pieces *out* of there, not *in*.

Sascha said the painting was used to clear up a debt. They continued the conversation, trying to figure out what the real story was about the location of the painting. Boris asked when Sascha was supposed to be back in town so they could clear up the information. He was due next week and Horst agreed to give Boris a call so they could talk to him together. Horst sensed that Boris had some suspicions and asked for him to share. Boris felt Sascha was getting off lightly because it seemed too convenient for the guy to disappear so easily.

Horst wasn't fully convinced, either way. The guy was a bit of a loner. He could have been a cop. Boris was resolute that it wasn't possible. Horst mostly agreed, but there was more to the story than anyone knew. Horst offered again for us to get high, but I wasn't in the mood even though I normally would have loved to.

"Go look, if you want," Horst noticed that I was interested in the paintings in the room. He had some nice fakes and interesting items. We talked about art comfortably, especially the art of forgery. He mentioned the piece by Fabritius. It was a unique piece.

Boris agreed and said that this was why they wanted it back. Horst spoke more about *The Goldfinch* and how Fabritius was making a pun on the art genre. The technique used was a joke at its heart to amuse the artist. Keeping that in mind, Horst felt that Fabritius was the best at it.

Horst had first seen the painting around the same age I had. His father had taken him to the Mauritshius where *The Goldfinch* was left in his memory as a piece of work most appealing to a child. Boris was getting bored with the art talk, but I continued with Horst, wondering if he dealt with modern art. He didn't exactly *deal* in the proper sense, but he said, "Sometimes". He asked the same of me, but I didn't very often because the paintings went to the art dealers before me.

We continued our talk until I got to what I thought was a Corot, but turned out to be Van Goyen. Horst brought it closer for me to look at. A young boy entered the room. Horst snapped Ulrika back to the kitchen as she came around with a couple of the prep-school kids.

Things started to get a weird and Boris got up, calling me with him. The walls started to move as hands and bodies began to move and appear. Boris made a stern and quick movement for us to get out. He yelled out a "Ciao," and pushed me out the door. The last thing I saw was one of the young boys being lifted up and given something from a syringe.

17

I was bewildered. I thought we should call 911, but Boris said no. He didn't want to wait for the car, even and called Gyuri to pick us up on the other side of the park. Boris told me not to worry, that the boy would be fine. I said they should take him to the ER, but Boris didn't agree. The boy will be fine, he assured.

It was dark already and after taking a call, Boris muttered something to himself. He tried to explain what had happened. Horst kept his place open to kids who would trade art or paintings for a high. The boys went there to have a safe place to explore. The adults knew how to help the kids be safe. Boris kept talking, trying to cheer me up, but I was still in a fog. Boris felt good that he had more information. I was startled out of my own thoughts.

Boris believed it was Sascha who had taken the painting. Sascha was Ulrika's brother. He and Horst were very close, so much so that he can't take any kind of criticism towards his brother. Boris always got along with Sascha, but not with his sister. Even though they got along, Boris was surprised at the idea that Sascha would go against Horst, who was whipped when it came to Sascha. Boris tried to describe the type of men Horst and Sascha were. He was concerned that he had no idea who the extra guy was that Sascha picked up.

I was starting to understand the work that Boris did. The painting could never be sold, but could be bartered with on the black market as if it were currency. People might trade the painting for a place to stay, cash, drugs, a girl or a boy. The point was that the painting would never be sold, but would continue to be used to trade with unless the cops found it, which they hadn't yet.

I said that I wanted the cops to find it. Boris said that I was noble, but that at the moment, the painting was just going to move around. He told me to not worry and to cheer up. Then, he was gone.

18

He took off saying he was late and didn't have time to take me home. I was so shaken by the whole experience that I had to pause to get my bearings. I was so distracted that I didn't know where to go. Kitsey's apartment was the closest. She stayed with two roommates and they should be out on their Girls' Night. I had a key and could relax there and wait for her to come home.

Normally, I would call before stopping in. I felt the safest at Kitsey's apartment, despite her roommates. No one knew how to find me there. Plus, she hadn't fully moved in, so I liked the sparse feeling of the place. I put my key in the door and unlocked it, only to be stopped by the chain. I was surprised and tried it again. I knocked loudly and waited for someone to answer.

It was Emily. She said Kitsey wasn't there and they didn't know when she'd be back. Emily and Kitsey had been friends since they were kids and I remembered her slamming a door on me at the Barbours'. She made it known that she didn't think I was good enough.

I asked her to let me in anyway so I could wait for her. Emily said it wasn't a good time just then. I started to get a bit annoyed, but Emily told me I had better come back later. I tried to persist in just being able to lie down in Kitsey's room, Emily insisted it was a bad time. She threw out that she lived there and that I didn't have the right to come barging in whenever. She apologized, telling me I should come back and closed the door.

19

I stood in the hallway. I could hear Emily breathing heavily on the other side of the door. I thought she would be taken off the bridesmaids list as I went down the stairs. I wondered why Emily wasn't with the others at the movies and if she had a guy in there. Outside, I stopped to check my messages and text Kitsey before heading downtown. If she was getting out of her movie we could meet up for dinner and drinks without her friends. I was also curious to get the scoop on Emily.

I sent a text with no response. I called, but it went to voicemail. I looked in the window reflection and saw her arm in arm with a familiar man, Tom Cable. He was carrying a bag from the wine shop where she and I often went. They were very much involved with each other. She had more affection and interest in him than she ever had in me. I was stunned. As they crossed the street, I watched them in the glass. Kitsey was upset and talking with emotion. He was soothing her and she was enjoying the loving attention. They walked right by me and I realized she was crying, something I'd never seen her do.

20

I barely slept that night and was preoccupied when I opened the store the next day. I even forgot to turn the sign to *Open* on the door for a half hour. Things were becoming clearer with Kitsey's twice a week trips to the Hamptons or strange numbers appearing on her phone, which she attributed to various other people calling her. Sometimes texts would come in the middle of the night and she would say it was the wrong number.

The most disappointing realization of all was in Mrs. Barbour's subtle ways of keeping the truth from me. It was clear that Mrs. Barbour knew what was going on, but couldn't tell me. We were meant to see each other that night for a birthday party of her friends and then go onto another party. Kitsey sent me a text, saying she was at work and to call. I hadn't decided what to do nor did I know what I could say to her.

Boris came bursting into the shop. He only had a moment to tell me some good news. He had a line on the painting. He didn't have more information than that. I tried to tell him that the painting needed to be handled carefully, not mistreated. Boris assured me that Horst had taken care of it beautifully, but he couldn't say with these guys he didn't know. He did say that he heard it was being kept in a restaurant or a building with one. There was more. Horst found out that my last name was Decker and called Boris asking if I knew someone called Lucius Reeve.

I sat down asking, "Why?"

Horst said to let me know to stay away from Reeve. He had connected the dots to the painting once he knew my name. I was being warned to stay away from Reeve because Horst had bad dealings with him before. Boris asked how I knew Reeve and I said it was complicated. Boris offered his help if I needed it and so did Horst. I had left a good impression on him. Boris had to run off and promised to speak soon.

As he was about to run off, I asked what he would do if his girl were cheating on him. He asked if I was sure or not. I said no, though that wasn't exactly true. He said, "In that case, ask her directly in when she's vulnerable and more willing to tell the truth." He asked me if she was beautiful, rich, intelligent and heartless. I nodded. He said I couldn't be too much in love then, because I wasn't wild or mad by the idea that she might be cheating. He said this was a good thing.

21

Kitsey knew something was up and wasn't as composed as usual. She was rambling about different things. She asked if I wanted to have curry, but I'd made up my mind to be angry with her, so I wasn't kind. She tried to keep things even, but said we could do what I wanted. That set me off. I told her she could stop pretending now and that I knew. She feigned ignorance. I told her that I'd seen her with Tom. She tried to play innocent, saying that they were really close friends and that he was friends with Emily, too. She said he felt awful about the way he treated me after my mom died. That killed me.

"You and Tom have been talking about me? Well, does his mother still have a place in East Hampton?" That was my way of letting her know that I knew who she was with when she was playing golf.

"I don't want to do this," she said, but I wasn't in the mood to let it go. I started my scenario about her and Tom. I knew they were seeing each other before we got together because Platt told me. Her parents didn't like Tom, so they pretended until Platt found out.

She suddenly said, "I won't see him anymore." She admitted to it and claimed that she didn't think it really mattered until we were married.

"Why would you think that?" I asked.

For the first time, I saw her get angry. She shouted that I was playing the victim, but that everyone had warned her about me, that I was hooked on drugs. She hadn't cared about that. She didn't want things to become mean, but the fact was that she was in love with Tom. She knew she couldn't be with him, though; and she knew I was a good match, and she said there was no reason to ruin what we had. She went on to point out how happy our relationship made her mother, and said we were such a good fit. We made a great match. All she wanted was for us to be good to each other and to enjoy our lives together.

22

In the end, I stayed. We ordered in and went to bed. It was easy to pretend that everything was fine but I still felt a heavy weight of something pressing down on us. There was a silence between us. It reminded me of my first not-so-much girlfriend, Julie. We hooked up, but neither of us would admit it and we'd never loved each other. That was what things with Kitsey had become.

23

Dealing with Kitsey helped me to forget about Boris, but those thoughts returned in my dreams. I was shocked awake. After trying to go back to sleep, I decided to get up. The dream seemed prophetic and I couldn't shake the feeling it left. To think of how much I'd worried about the painting when I thought it was safely stored in my temperature controlled rented storage locker. Now, I didn't even know where it was, or where it had been over the past several years, and the stress on my mind was far too heavy to bear. How long, exactly, had Boris had the painting, or even Horst, the one who loved art so much.

Nothing good could come from this situation. Kitsey's phone wasn't where it normally was at night. I was used to seeing the blue light, showing a message in the middle of the night. What did she and Tom talk about? I could imagine them happily together. My thoughts went back to the painting. Of all I'd lost in my life, this left me unmoored more than anything.

24

Not being able to go back to sleep, I quietly left Kitsey's place. I arrived back at Hobie's place and heard a voice from the kitchen. I was surprised to hear it and saw a red head poke around the corner. I was so surprised to see her that I had no words. I could hardly believe she was there, saying that she'd missed me.

I stuttered, asking what she was doing there. She explained that she was going to Montreal on her way to meet Everett in California. The flight was re-routed and she was in Newark. She figured that she might as well come for a quick visit. I was surprised as she kissed me hello and congratulated me on my upcoming marriage. She was asking when she was going to meet Kitsey and kept talking, ignoring the fact that I wasn't saying anything back.

All I could manage again was to ask where Hobie had gone off to. He'd run to get some pastries that she loved even though she told him not to worry about it. She kept buzzing about and said she'd made some CDs for me but hadn't brought them because she hadn't known she was going to be visiting. I said I had some for her, too. In fact, I had a lot of things for her. Since I thought about her all the time, I often found things I thought she would like, books, jewelry, perfume and anything else.

I said I was going to stop in my room for a minute and she said she'd be in the kitchen. I returned to normal breath and thought after I closed the door to my room. I thought about taking a shower or cleaning up, but I realized that I would be wasting my precious time with her. I opened the door and yelled down the hall, inviting her out to a movie with me that night. I mentioned a Glenn Gould documentary I'd already seen, but lied, saying I hadn't. She said, "Sounds fantastic. What time?"

25

At work, I was full of excitement for the day to end. With every free moment, I was thinking about what to wear, where to take her to dinner and what we could talk about. Around six, Hobie came home from spending the day with Pippa and popped his head in the store. Of course, he knew that Pippa and I were going out that night. It was obvious how I felt about her and I was sure that Hobie knew, but he never said anything. He told me that he'd left Pippa to do some Christmas shopping and that she would meet me. He mentioned the film, knowing that I'd already seen it, but confirmed that he didn't tell her that. He offered to watch the shop so that I could get ready to go.

26

I was happier than I'd ever been, or at least in a long while, on my way to meet Pippa. It took me a moment to gather myself when I saw her, so I didn't seem overly eager. We got popcorn and headed into the theater, together. I knew all of her little likes and dislikes from probing Hobie over the years with questions about her. The theater was more crowded than I preferred, but it didn't matter just then. As we watched the movie, I kept trying to look at her. About half an hour in, I realized she was upset. The rest of the film left me feeling miserable, anxious about upsetting her.

27

As we left the theater, I apologized for the film upsetting her. She seemed surprised and I told her we could have left had she wanted to. She said that it wasn't that she didn't enjoy the film. For a moment, my mind raced around what to do next and if we should go to dinner or if she wanted to go home. I suggested that we go near Bedford Street, which had cafes and nice places to eat get a drink.

28

Amazingly, the Gods were in my favor because the place that we found was just right. We had a cozy table with our faces lit with candlelight. There was quiet Bob

Dylan playing in the background and it was the perfect setting. Pippa was asking me all kinds of questions. We shared our medical treatments since we were both diagnosed with PTSD. She told me about life in Europe and how she wanted a dog, but couldn't have one.

She mentioned that she'd missed me and that I looked better than I had for a long time. We stayed there, laughing and talking for hours. It became more and more clear how much I loved her. She was talking about the film again. Welty had seen Glenn Gould play at Carnegie. She had really liked the movie. What had upset her were the concert scenes. She'd spent so many hours all those years ago, practicing and she hadn't been able to go back to it after the explosion.

I already knew about this from Hobie who talked to Aunt Margaret a great deal about things. Aunt Margaret had no idea, sending her to some strange school in Europe. She complained that she could listen to music on her iPod, but hadn't been to a concert in years. I asked her why, but I knew. The crowds bothered her like they did me. I told her she could get medication or use hypnosis, but she said those wouldn't work for the negative emotions that she had. She didn't know they made a drug for that. Due to the anxiety, she didn't work. Luckily, she didn't have to. Unfortunately, Everett was the same, only he had to work, just not as long as he was with Pippa.

Pippa tried being a teacher of music, but it wasn't for her. She didn't know what else she could do to stay near music and not be able to play it. She didn't like living in London either. She didn't know what to do. I told her to come home. She asked about Everett, but I didn't answer and she confirmed how much I didn't like him. She explained that if I got to know him, I would.

I stayed silent. Pippa admitted to having thought about moving back to New York. She missed Hobie and he had joked about getting her an apartment for the same price they spent on phone calls. Hobie tried to get her to move back, but not with direct words.

Then, she told me something she hadn't told a lot of people. The reason she stays away so much is to avoid the memories of where she used walk or play music or had dinner with Welty and Hobie. Being back reminded her of how everything stopped for her after the explosion. She said she'd even stopped growing after the accident, which is fairly normal to people who are injured and traumatized as children. Pippa gave an example of a Saudi princess who was kidnapped when she was 12 and never grew anymore.

I took her hand easily as we talked. She knew that I understood the thoughts of what if we hadn't been there that particular day. I told her how I go through that, too. Then, she said how if we hadn't been there that day, we might never have met. She asked me what I thought I would be doing now if everything hadn't changed back then. I was surprised by the question and didn't know.

We talked about how strange it seems to blame ourselves for not being able to predict the future, but her doctor had told that there was something like 75% of victims are sure there were signs they should have known. She began to cry as she recalled that day and how she had insisted on Welty coming with her uptown to take her to lunch before her audition. I told her that he had known what he was doing. She looked at me as if I had just said the wrong thing, but I knew it wasn't.

I shared how he'd been talking about her the whole time and how sharing someone's last moments on earth sort of makes you merge into that person. Then, I shared with her an experience I'd had with a woman named Barbara Guibbory who gave seminars on past-life-regression, reincarnation and karmic ties. One evening, I'd been out with Hobie and she came to me out of the blue saying that I was unrooted, had a constriction of the heart and a fragmented energy field.

Hobie asked her what about him. She told him that he was an Advanced Being. Welty had been too. Pippa mentioned how Everett had also studied about this, which annoyed me, but I continued. My point was that ever since that day, Welty had been a part of me. It seemed like the only way to explain how things had turned out ever since coming to stay with Hobie. I had no interest in antiques or knowledge of how to run the shop, but I was doing it.

I concluded with how weird it was that Welty sent me to the house and that it was as if he'd sent me to be who I needed to be and with those I needed to be with. She looked at me, not like Kitsey did with half-attention, but with full attention and understanding. She had a sadness in her expression that seemed only worse because she did like me and we did connect on many levels. She understood and didn't like the misery that I felt over her.

29

The magic of the night before was gone the next day, the day of my engagement party. We were awkward around each other. It reminded me of the time when just before she brought home Everett, we sat on the stoop, talking and talking, forming a bond over our shared interests and thoughts. We had gone back inside and lost all the magic, leaving us embarrassed and awkward around each other. I wanted that to come back and it had. Now everything was back to the way it always was. I tried to be content with that, but I wasn't.

30

Our party was being hosted by Kitsey's godmother in a private club that Hobie knew about, but had never visited. Pippa was going to attend and asked how many people would be there. I said a couple of hundred and only 15 of that was for me. Hobie added that all the important people of the city, state and even the Prince of Monaco would be there.

I was just making my appearance and doing what I was told. Anne de Larmessin, Kitsey's godmother, was really the one in charge. She had taken on the role of mother-of-the-bride for Mrs. Barbour due to the distress after the deaths of Andy and Mr. Barbour. She made herself indispensable when it came to anything regarding our wedding. The best part of the whole thing was that Anne de Larmessin was so disturbed by me as the least desirable match for Kitsey. She wouldn't even say my name. I just went by *the groom*.

31

There was no reason for me to be alert at the party, so I loaded myself up and took a few backup oxys with me. The club was beautiful. I hated that there were so many people there to prevent me from fully appreciating the architecture and portraits. I just stood around, dazed and not wanting to be there. Pippa came up to me, asking what was wrong. I looked sad. I said that I *was sad*. Just as I said it, Hobie came up pressing me to attend to the guests.

I hesitated, and he told me not to worry. I braced myself and went among the crowd. Mrs. Barbour caught me as she was trying to get away from some man, talking about something or other. She introduced me to him, Havistock Irving. Mr. Irving knew Hobie and Welty.

He was a direct descendent of Washington Irving and felt his ancestors would approve of his work in libraries, reading old papers and studying historical government records. Then, a bomb was dropped. His close associate was none other than Lucius Reeve. The room faded into the background. He brought up the chest-on-chest item of dispute between us, though cordially.

I restated my interest in buying the piece back, but he responded that Lucius wasn't interested in that, hinting to a more interesting piece available. Pleasantly, I told him that business could be forgotten. To which, Irving replied that he didn't see that happening. I smiled in response. He made an undercutting threat about his and Lucius' awareness of other pieces I'd sold and how he wondered if the buyers even knew about how interesting their pieces really were. I tried to keep a steady expression as he said that after the holidays were over, Lucius intended to follow up on some of the bigger pieces I'd sold. Kitsey walked up and Irving greeted her. He cozied up to her and suggested they go off somewhere quiet where he could give her all the gossip on me.

31

Mrs. Barbour was relieved as he exited the conversation. She said that the chatter was making her tired and how surprised she was at all the people there. It looked like they'd known each other for quite some time, but he had a familiar way with everyone. They met from some volunteer work for the New York Historical Society. She said she didn't buy his connection to Washington Irving at all. There was really no proof either way.

It did seem, , that he was very much aware of all the gossip, historical and current. Suddenly, Mrs. Barbour felt tired and hungry. I offered a seat and suggested I get something for her to eat, but she didn't want me to leave her. I told her it wouldn't take long and that I'd bring back something for her quickly.

I went to find Hobie, but Platt caught up with me, already half drunk, before I could reach Hobie. He asked if Kitsey and I had cleared things up. I wasn't sure how to respond, but he informed me that Tom didn't love her and that I was the best thing to happen to her and she knew it. He blabbered on about how poorly Tom had treated her and how his whole family didn't like the way Tom behaved, but she was and is still crazy for him.

Platt tried to get me to be content with the fact that she was at least marrying me. He continued to say that nothing would have worked between Kitsey and Tom. Still, I informed him that she had admitted to loving Tom. Platt was about to get us both to a drink, but I said I had to speak to someone and suggested that he should look after his mother. Then, he was off.

33

When I caught up with Hobie, he had a worried look, based on my expression. I wanted to have a moment with him, but I got mobbed by strangers who were having their first glimpse of me. Hobie introduced me to the group and I pulled him aside as tactfully as possible. I asked him if he knew a man named Havistock Irving. He didn't seem to recognize the name, but looked concerned about me, so I must have looked bad or maybe he understood my mental state better than I knew.

Hobie didn't know the name. I explained the best I could about Irving, but Hobie had no knowledge of him.

When I pointed him out in the mob of people, Hobie recognized him, but wouldn't say that they knew each other. They had crossed paths and he'd used a different name when he and Welty knew him: Sloane Griscam. No one knew his true name.

He was known as a knocker, or someone who charmed his way into the homes of the elderly and tried to cheat or sometimes rob them. This was just the kind of place one would expect to see Irving cum Griscam. His partner, Lucian Race, was also quite the scammer, according to Hobie. The two had a whole routine worked out and would carry out their scams.

Irving or Griscam would initiate contact and charm his way into an invite to the home of some well-to-do man or woman or couple. He would arrive with his good friend, Lucian Race, or Lucius Reeve, and while Irving distracted them, Reeve would pilfer anything of value. I could tell that some other people wanted to come engage either me or Hobie in conversation, but I was not yet done talking to Hobie privately. He looked for an opportunity to change the subject and asked if I'd eaten anything. I lied that I had.

I continued asking how he and Welty had crossed paths with Irving and Reeve. Irving had come to the shop trying to sell what he claimed were family items. Welty recognized a piece and knew who he'd sold it to. He also knew that a couple of knockers had conned her and taken items from her. Welty accepted the pieces on consignment and called the police.

For Hobie's side, he was swindled by Irving by buying in full an *estate,* which had actually been his hideout for stolen items. In the end, they were taken to court. Irving had completely vanished, but Reeve spent some time in jail. This had all happened about 30 to 35 years ago. I asked about Race, as Hobie had known him. He described the man I knew as Lucius Reeve. Finally, a couple managed to get over to us, so Hobie ended the conversation by introducing me to them.

34

From six to nine, I managed to survive the party, making small talk with this person or that person. I hardly saw Hobie and Pippa. Even Kitsey would dart in, introduce someone to me and then dart away. Luckily, I didn't have to face Irving again. Finally, people were starting to clear out when I saw Pippa across the room with Boris. I made my way to them and said how happy I was to see him.

Pippa and Boris had already acquainted themselves, and Boris needed to talk to me privately. Boris thought that Pippa was the one I was marrying, but I corrected him. He realized then that she was the one I loved, but asked for my fiancée. I pointed out Kitsey to him. He exclaimed at her beauty but outer coldness. I agreed. He confirmed that she was the one I asked about. He saw that I hadn't been satisfied by her admittance of the truth. He paused and said that I had to tell her that I needed to leave.

I asked why, not wanting to leave Pippa. He said I would feel great when I heard what he had to say. He told me I needed to go home, get my passport and probably some cash. I started to drift off, seeing people around the room. Boris brought me back to reality and said we would talk in the car and that we needed to go. He had a ticket for me. I was in a daze. What was he saying?

He said I shouldn't worry because everything was fine. I just had to figure out a way to be gone for a couple of days or three at most. He shoved me off to go arrange it. He asked about the money I had on me. I mentioned the bank and he said that wouldn't do. He was in a hurry and pressed me to make a move.

35

As I approached Kitsey, she affectionately kissed me, just in time for the flash of a photo. She chattered about the party and drew in her aunt to get a group photo of the three of us. I stopped her and said that I was going. She was confused and said how a table had been booked, but I said firmly that I wouldn't make it. I told her to say that I was taking her mother home since we both knew she wouldn't be going out. I told her she could figure it out.

Kitsey thought I was upset or vexed with her. I said I wasn't. The thing with Tom Cable meant nothing, now that we'd settled our situation. She'd chosen to wear my mother's earrings, I noticed. I also realized she was right, that they didn't suit her at all. I reached out and touched them and her on the cheek. Those watching were moved by the seemingly touching action.

Taking advantage of the photographic moment, Kitsey played it nice. She agreed to cover my absence and asked when I would return. I just said soon, but I would like to never return. I told her to take care and to not let Havistock Irving in her mother's house.

She hesitated, then said he'd been annoying lately with constant calls of wanting to visit or bringing flowers and chocolates. Her mother wouldn't see him, but Kitsey felt sorry for him. I told her to have no pity on him and keep him away, warning that he was sharper than he let on. With that, I gave her another photographic kiss and went to tell Hobie that I needed to leave for a bit.

He seemed cautious, wondering if it were me and Kitsey going away somewhere, but I said no. He looked at Boris and said, "You know, if you need anything, you can always ask." I thanked him and he turned back to the portrait he'd been looking at. I shook Hobie's hand as I went to go. Pippa wasn't anywhere in sight, so I couldn't say goodbye to her. I asked Hobie if he knew where she'd gone, but he didn't know. I paused at the coat check for a few minutes, hoping to catch her, until Boris grabbed me and pulled me out the door.

Part Five

We have art in order not to die from the truth. –
NIETZSCHE

Chapter Eleven: Amsterdam

1

The car was circling the block, but the driver wasn't Gyuri. It was Anatoly, another Russian who didn't speak any English. I asked about Gyuri and Boris said he'd flown over the day before.

"Fly? Fly where?" I asked.

"Antwerp."

"My painting's there?"

"No, but my apartment is there and my car. Gyuri is picking up the car and some other things to meet us."

Boris handed me a ticket from Newark to Amsterdam. It was only a three-hour drive from Antwerp to Amsterdam. We were on different flights, but we would all arrive around the same time at the same place. Mine was direct, leaving tonight. I asked why I was going.

Boris said that he may need some help and didn't want to bring anyone else in on the activity except Gyuri. He hadn't even told Myriam, who booked the tickets, what was going on. He said he could have, as he did trust her, but the fewer people who knew, the better. He pushed me along. I needed to get my passport and all the cash I could get. Then, Anatoly would take us to the airport.

Boris was packed and ready, so he waited for me in the car. I asked about the money. Boris said I just needed some cash and that mostly it was for show. I was confused. He explained how he planned to pay them. There was no way Boris was going to reward them for stealing from him. He said the man was weak and he'd teach him a lesson, but in the meantime he wanted them to think that we would pay the full price. Boris suggested I could stop at an ATM and get some money or maybe at the airport.

He cautioned that I could only take $10,000 in currency to the EU, but he had more in his carry case hidden away. Furthermore, he said that I shouldn't have to foot the whole amount, so his gift to me was to give me some when we arrived.

His plan was to offer them a bank draft instead of cash, but most people wouldn't accept that. He just didn't know how things were going to work out, so we would play it by ear. He felt that they were inexperienced and desperate, so he crossed his fingers and said, "I'm hopeful. We will see!"

2

While Boris waited with Anatoly, driving around the block, I grabbed some unbanked cash from the shop, which was around $16,000 and then quickly packed some things including my passport. Momentarily, I picked up my tin of opiates, but dropped it and quickly shut the drawer. Popper was running around with me anxiously. I paused when I saw Pippa's green boots outside her door and went back to get the first edition of the book, *Ozma of Oz*, and jotted a note: *Safe trip. I love you. No kidding.*

I tucked it in the book and placed it next to her boots. I paused to take in the significance of that moment, where I told her exactly how I felt, and briefly recalling our lovely moments together. I went back to my room to get the necklace I bought for her and draped it over the boots. It was an 18th century topaz, made for a fairy queen. It was the perfect shade of her eyes. With a feeling of both fear and excitement I ran out. Hobie would know what it cost me, but Pippa would find all of it long after I was gone.

3

Our flights were in different terminals, so we said goodbye at the curb. I entered the airport and walked past the shops, stopping only at the Duty Free where I bought a fifth of vodka. I headed down to my gate, which was crowded with other waiting passengers. It was a full flight and I wondered how Myriam had gotten me a seat at all. I was too tired to care too much and slept through the entire flight, waking up only for the pre-landing breakfast. Boris and I arranged to meet in the baggage claim. I waited there for an hour, though I had no luggage checked. Finally, Boris arrived and we went to meet Gyuri.

4

With the suddenness of the trip, I hadn't expected all of the Christmas decorations everywhere. Myriam booked a hotel in the old part of town. I checked in and locked away the cash before meeting Boris again while Gyuri parked the car. Boris was hungry, so we began to walk. He mentioned that it had been a while since he'd been there. He looked both out of place and at home on the streets of Amsterdam.

We popped in to a side bar or café along the canal. It wasn't the nicest of places and the menu was on a chalkboard with items I couldn't make out. Boris offered to order and spoke easy Dutch. Boris was telling me stories of when he'd been there before, but I was so overwhelmed that I didn't hear much as I tried to take in the city. Gyuri eventually joined us and we caught up a bit.

Boris had moved on to talk about Horst, saying he didn't know why the man didn't live in Amsterdam since he hates New York so much. I asked if Horst knew that we were here. Boris said no. It was easier in the long run. Boris' suspicions of Horst's man, Sascha, were correct. Sascha was the one to steal the painting in the first place. Since he was Ulrika's brother, Boris felt it would be better to take care of things himself and that way, Horst would owe him later.

I asked for clarification. Boris said he would give me the short story. I asked if Ulrika knew about her brother stealing the painting, but that was unclear. Gyuri voiced his doubts. I suggested that if it was already known who had the painting, then we could just call the police. It wasn't the actual police that I meant, but the art-crimes people. They could take care of the recovery completely. Boris said it wasn't a good idea. I tried to tell him how easy and simple it would be to get someone else to do it.

Gyuri told me to eat. I offered to make the call. Boris snapped at that and told me not to call and to shut up about the whole idea. Gyuri put his hand on my wrist and I understood the meaning of the gesture. Boris continued about how I should put the idea out of my head and then went back to talking about Sascha.

I stopped and decided that I could make the call myself without either of them knowing. I asked where the painting was, but Boris didn't know. The other party wasn't about to tell us. A meeting was to be set up, but it hadn't been yet. They were changing the location many times out of paranoia. Boris wanted to set up the meet at my hotel and bring me in as the super rich American interested in buying the painting. They wanted to choose location.

With that, Boris asked if I knew where my hotel was. I thought I did. I asked where he and Gyuri were staying, but they were vague. Boris said they would meet me at my hotel and we had each other's numbers.

5

I ended up wandering the streets of Amsterdam for several hours, having made a wrong turn at some point. There was a lot to see and I felt overwhelmed, exhausted and cold. I finally got directions to get back. Arriving in my room, I collapsed on the bed and slept. My phone rang to wake me up and I forgot for a moment that I wasn't home. It was Boris. He was coming up.

6

Although Boris had said he was coming up, he made it to my door rather quickly, considering where my room was situated in the hotel. He told me to clean up and get the money I brought. As I was finishing up, I walked into the room to see Boris checking a gun. This unnerved me even though Boris claimed it was all for show and he had no intention of using it. When I looked at Gyuri, he showed no signs of anything.

Boris justified it by saying that we were meeting them on their turf and that it would be expected that he and Gyuri carry a gun as my bodyguards. I said I couldn't do it. The gun's presence changed everything.

"Can't what?" Boris asked. My only job was to stand for five minutes and pretend so that he could get the painting back for me. I continued to feel extremely uncomfortable with a bad feeling about the whole thing. I simply said, "I can't."

Boris would hear none of it. I told him we should have talked about it all before we got to this point. Boris shut me down again and told me to listen, get ready and do the meet; then, we'd have the painting and everyone would be happy. Gyuri said something to Boris in Ukrainian and Boris agreed. I needed to look richer and more believable for their story. Gyuri gave me his Platinum Rolex President and bevel-cut diamond ring. Once I looked close enough, they put together the money in the briefcase.

7

We were in the car, passing the Christmas frenzy outside, as Boris was talking about the meet. He set up a bank draft and hoped that the sellers were in enough of a hurry to get rid of the painting that they would be willing to accept just about anything. Gyuri and Boris appeared at ease and offered to tell me the plan, now that I was already in the car. We were taking the car out the city to a garage where we were to meet Cherry, or Victor, and he would drive us to the meeting place.

Cherry was the one who set up the meeting. I confirmed that it was all meant to be peaceful, still very concerned about the gun. Boris was upbeat about it. We were in an area called Overtoom, not that nice to look at, but Boris' contact had a garage there and that's where they were storing the car.

Boris told me to give him my passport, which made me nervous. He put his and Gyuri's in the glove box along with mine. That made me nervous, but Boris figured it was better to get caught without an ID than it was to get caught with it in this kind of situation.

8

Once we arrived and parked, I met Victor. He introduced us to his friend, Shirley T, given the nickname for his dimpled-cheeks. We all made our greetings and got in his car. He said it should be an easy meeting. They were all convinced that they were doing Sascha some kind of favor by getting the painting off his hands, since he'd stolen from Horst.

For Sascha, according to them, the painting was about getting enough money to feed his habits. Victor had been able to push things more in our favor due to their indecisiveness with the location. This was meant to help us on the money side of things, they would be willing to accept the bank draft since I was in a hurry and they had delayed our meeting. At least that was what the group thought. He told us the location was a Lunch café called *De Paarse Koe*, which meant the Purple Cow in Dutch.

It wasn't an attractive place to dine, but the location was remote, which is what they wanted. I started to tune them out and they began speaking in Russian until Boris translated for me. They confirmed that Sascha wasn't going to be at the meeting, which was good because it meant that Boris could be inside with me. Next, they began to tell me my story. I was an art dealer based in New York who had spent some time in jail for forgery and was running a similar operation to Horst's on a smaller scale.

Victor told Boris to give me the bank draft and deposit slip, as I should be the one who gives it to them. Boris didn't seem pleased, but he handed it over and I took a look at it. My name was Farruco Frantisek? What?

Boris defended it saying that he didn't choose it. It was just the best he could get in the circumstances. I practiced it so that it came out naturally. As we continued towards the meeting, I tried to find a focal point to center myself. The only thing I could refer to was the moon.

9

Truly, the Purple Cow left much to be desired in terms of location, design and décor. Boris saw me checking it out all and promised that in 20 minutes we would be on our way to a really nice dinner. He wasn't going in yet, but told me to go with Victor and Gyuri.

A man came to the front door of the café and hesitated, as if unsure about letting us in. A second guy appeared. The first guy was making a call and another one was agitated. He returned to the door and let us in. As soon as we were inside, he began talking to Victor rapidly.

While they talked, I stood around, nonchalantly. Boris slipped in next to me to translate. We were on time, but one of their guys hadn't shown and they wanted us to wait. Boris said to let Victor handle it. Finally, they came towards me and I introduced myself as Farruco.

Victor was looking at me to give him the papers. I started to hand them over when all of a sudden, Victor hit the man upside the head. I turned to see what happened to the second guy and was momentarily confused as to why he hadn't moved. Then, I saw that both Boris and Gyuri had guns on him.

I noticed a young Asian woman or boy in the kitchen, watching fearfully. I mentioned that someone was in the back. It wasn't clear if anyone heard me or not, but Cherry was too busy with the first guy he had tied up and carried to the kitchen.

The second guy threatened us, but Boris didn't seem too worried. The guy claimed to know who we were, but Boris didn't care about that either. Victor came out of the kitchen alone and bent to cuff the second guy. Boris told me to go get in the car and I did. A few seconds later, everyone was in the car and we sped off.

While I was wondering what had just happened, the rest of the guys were laughing, high-fiving and feeling good. Boris turned to me and explained that they'd made a last minute change of plans when the third man hadn't shown up. I was focused on the fact that they'd used guns, but Boris pointed out that no one had gotten hurt, so it didn't matter. I wanted to know why we hadn't just paid the money. Boris said it was because we lucked out. We had an opportunity to get away with the painting without having to pay for it. It was then that I mentioned the kid that I saw. No one else had seen her or him. Boris seemed curious, because I said she or he was Asian looking, though I didn't know which one exactly.

They sort of laughed it off and got sidetracked about other aspects of what had just gone down. They felt that they'd had a narrow miss since if the third guy had shown, things might have turned out quite differently. With that, they presented me with the gift of the painting. Boris asked where Cherry had found it. They had stashed it in a dirty broom closet in a plastic briefcase.

I was in a daze. Boris was telling me that he was giving the money they kept to Gyuri and Shirley T for their help that night. For Victor, they had some previous debt that was now fulfilled. Victor was telling a story of how Boris saved his life, but I was focused on the package in my lap. I was speechless. They teased me about wanting to phone the art cops.

11

When we arrived back at the garage, they were still celebrating the success of the meeting on their end, but I was still quiet and in shock. Boris joked that I looked like I had just had the best blowjob of my life. They all laughed, but I was stunned and trembling.

Boris told me to wrap up the painting and we'd put it in the hotel safe. The other guys wanted dinner. They agreed to meet in an hour at some place called Blake's. Victor was telling Shirley and Gyuri that they were buying dinner with their winnings for the night.

Gyuri momentarily was preoccupied with the money, wanting to divide it. He was a little worried that if one of them had all of it, then the other would not get his share. They agreed to drive together back into the city while Boris would take me in his car. Gyuri confirmed that this was okay and Boris insisted. Just as they pulled away, Boris hesitated, but it was too late.

12

Boris told me to tie up the painting better with the string I had brought. He took a look at the first, and we enjoyed it for a moment. He asked if it had been worth it. It had. Boris reminded me that if I did want to sell it, he could help me with that and I would be able to retire. That wasn't what I wanted and he understood. As I was trying to finish tying it up, Boris got impatient and did it for me.

13

Just as we were about to get into the car with the painting all tied up, we heard an American voice say, "Merry Christmas." There were three men and they were talking to Boris, not me. Just in front of them was the Asian boy that I'd seen at the café. Boris recognized one of the men as Martin. They greeted each other and seemed to be friendly. The second guy easily went up to Boris and relieved him of his gun. I was a little confused, but Martin kept speaking politely.

Boris asked what he was doing there and Martin said he was surprised that he'd received a call from Horst. Sascha had called Horst and told him that someone had taken the painting from him. As Martin went to take the painting from Boris, Boris gave me a look that I knew from earlier years. It meant that I should run for it.

I was too exhausted and shocked, and I told Boris to just give it to him. As Frits, the second guy, stepped forward with a gun to Boris's head, Martin took the painting and thanked him. It was obvious that Martin was high. He told Frits to take us to the corner of the garage. Now, I understood why Boris told me to run.

When Frits had turned his attention to me, Boris flung his cigarette at him. The box hit him in the face and landed in his shirt collar. Martin turned to see and we heard three fast cracks. We both turned, just in time for a fourth crack and then my face was splattered by blood off of the car roof. As my vision cleared, I saw the Asian boy looking horrified, with a bloody hand he was trying to wipe off on his shirtfront.

Boris was on the ground, but I couldn't tell if he was hurt or not. I instinctively ran over to him to find blood everywhere. Frits was more than dead. Before I knew it, Martin was over us and trying to get his gun up. What happened next was so fast that I hardly knew what I was doing. Somehow I had got my hands on the pistol and had started shooting. The kick back was surprising and made my shots flail. I got Martin in the shoulder and as he was falling, I shot him in the head.

He went down and I heard feet behind me. I saw the boy running up the exit ramp with the painting. I didn't have enough awareness to go after him. Instead, I dropped the gun and threw up. I was doubled over in shock. Boris slapped me out of it and tried to get me moving. He said it was over and that I'd saved us, but I couldn't focus. He was trying to clean things up to make it look like it was a drug-related shooting. I could see that he'd hurt his arm and focused my attention on that, even though he waved me off about it. Boris said he should have listened to me when I mentioned the Asian person in the back. The Asian boy was Sascha's boyfriend.

We made it into a bathroom in the parking garage and Boris dunked his head under the sink to wash off the blood. He told me to do the same. The ice coldness of the water helped to rouse me from my stupor. Boris was quickly trying to make me move looking at what I needed to hide. He said I should get rid of the coat, but it was too cold, so we turned it inside out instead.

I asked him again about his arm, but he said it was fine. We headed back to the car. He told me to get in and then it dawned on him that he couldn't really drive, but there was no way that I could in my current state. We got in the car with Boris behind the wheel. He managed to get us out of the garage and said I needed to help him with street signs, keep him out of bus lanes and things like that. Boris focused on driving as safely as possible so that the police didn't stop us. That was the last thing we needed. As he drove, Boris asked if I understood what had just happened. I didn't. He explained that Frits and Martin were Horst's guys. What Boris wasn't sure about was whether or not Horst was in on it from the beginning. Maybe he didn't know, but Sascha called. It wasn't clear, but Boris was replaying the night.

As we entered the city, the roads were blocked here and there. I was starting to panic about what happened. Boris would drop the gun in the canal and it couldn't be traced back to anyone in the group. Gyuri would change the car. We were safe.

I asked about the painting. It was gone, perhaps for good. He was upset about that, but after what happened to Sascha's boyfriend, he wouldn't want to be involved, since he wasn't even legal. He told me it might be easiest if we split up. I could probably walk to my hotel faster and wait for him there. He said we might not be able to talk for a bit and to not try to contact him. He would contact me as soon as he could. He also gave me a little bit of something to keep me calm. He warned not to take too much of it, though, then told me to go. As I got out, he was on his phone talking to Cherry in Ukrainian.

14

I didn't follow Boris' directions and wandered around the canal rings much longer than I should have. I was freezing and my clothes and hair were soaked. Since it was dark, it was hard to make out the streets, but good for not drawing attention to the blood on my clothes or how awful I looked. When I finally found the hotel, it was locked, with no one at the front desk. Luckily, the man from the desk came around the corner and quickly let me in while surreptitiously giving me an odd look. I tried to explain that I got caught in the rain and spilled chocolate on my shirt to explain my state.

After managing to get to my room, I got in the shower right away and tried to wash out the bloodstains from my shirt and coat. No matter how hard I tried, the shirt was a loss. The scarf and jacket were dark enough to hide the stains, but my coat was another story. I tried what I could to get the stains out.

I hung the clothes to dry, recalling the time I saw Boris' father's clothes hanging in the bathroom. I spent some time cleaning traces of the blood from the bathroom tile and tub. I used every towel they had. Finally, I washed myself and let myself go under the hot spray.

15

Hours later, a buzzing at my door jolted me awake. I thought it would be Boris, but when I opened the door, it was a maid offering to take my laundry. I was confused at first, but recalled that the deskman had offered to send someone to collect my laundry the night before. I quickly grabbed the suit jacket, scarf and a different shirt to give to her. Once she had gone, I lay back down, then jumped up worrying that it had been a bad idea to send out the laundry. It was too late to get it back.

16

The stuff Boris gave me was strong and his warning was appropriate. I was startled out of my bliss by the doorbell again. My clothes were back from the laundry. I stopped worrying and let housekeeping see me in my bathrobe, locked out of my room as I'd gone to ask them to refresh my towels. I wasn't worried when I ordered room service for a few days or wore all the clothes I had with me or drank and ate everything from the minibar. With the help of Boris' dope, I dreamt of Andy. He came to say goodbye to me. I tried to go with him, but I couldn't.

17

The drug was wearing off and I woke up feeling horrible. I managed to get to the bathroom to be sick. I finally noticed the clean laundry and took off the plastic to inspect for any traces of blood. They seemed fine. I was delirious from the drug or from being ill. I dreamt of my father, saying, *There's always more to things, a hidden level. There's a pattern and we're a part of it.*

Chapter Twelve: Coming Home

1

For the next several days up to Christmas, I stayed in the room, trying to recover from the sickness that was now consuming me. Sometimes I watched TV, but I ordered room service and asked for Dutch newspapers, trying to see if there was anything about the murders. There were articles, but they were calling it a drug altercation.

One night I managed to sneak out to get a few things at a little Asian-run market near the hotel. I got cleaning supplies in hopes of cleaning up the shirt, but nothing I did could salvage it. I gave up and determined to get rid of it somehow. I really had no idea how many days it had been since I'd arrived in Amsterdam. My situation reminded me of my father. I could see him pacing up and down the room, enjoying the drama of the situation.

I had a fever and would dream of memories of my father, of being a child, of Mr. Barbour, of the old apartment on 7th Avenue and other random thoughts. Finally, I thought of Boris. I wondered what to do. I'd heard nothing from him. It had been too long. I was worried something had happened to him.

He'd texted me his number before we left the States, so I took comfort in knowing that I could text him if I wanted to. At some point, I caved and decided to text him, *Where are you?* I saw that my phone battery had died and went to the front desk for a charger. When I plugged it in, the phone began to charge, but crashed. It was damaged that night, but seemed fine later. Plugging it in was the last straw. Now, I didn't have Boris' number at all and no phone. I also had no return ticket home, though I did have a credit card. I figured I could always get a cab to the airport and then buy my own ticket or call Mrs. Barbour's assistant to help me get one.

It was nice to think normally again. I began to wonder more what happened to Boris and thought that maybe I shouldn't leave after all in case something happened to him. It was then that I recalled that I'd left my passport in Boris' glove box.

Calmly, I tried to think of all the steps that would be required for me to get a new passport. It was a lot more trouble than I was currently prepared for. I realized that there was no passport control in the European Union countries, via train. Where would I go, though, on the train? A million different questions and scenarios were running through my mind. There was too much to think of.

2

On Christmas Eve day, I ordered in a huge breakfast from room service and made up my mind. I headed out to Central Station in hopes of being able to get a ticket on the train. I waited in line for a long time to get to the ticket counter. The woman asked for my passport. I said that it was stolen and all I had was my New York State ID, credit cards and my social security card. The woman wouldn't budge on the fact that I needed a passport, no matter what kind of story I gave her.

I finally gave up and walked out when a teenager came up to warn to not try getting on the train without a passport. He said that most of the time no one checks, but if you were caught without one, it wasn't worth it. He was probably right. I headed to a payphone so I could call the US Consulate in hopes of them helping me.

From a pay phone, I made the call. A nice American voice came on. I told her my passport had been stolen and I needed a new one. She explained that I needed a police report, which should get delivered to them. From there, she gave me the list of things I would need to be able to get my passport. The main thing was that it would take a while to actually get the passport since it was the holidays. What was I supposed to do?

3

My fever would return at night. It was going up after being out in the cold for so long. I made it back to the hotel and warmed myself up. Suddenly, a strange feeling came over me. I'd had it before. It was a darkness that started to take over. Why was I still alive?

I thought of just turning myself in, but somehow ending my life seemed more hopeful. I wasn't sure that I had enough dope left to take care of the job and it frightened me to think about waking up in a Dutch hospital with no passport. I knew my tolerance had gone down, so maybe there was enough with the help of the Oxy I had and all the booze in the mini-bar. Once I made a decision about it, I was calm. Taking advantage of this feeling, I began to write my goodbye letters. I wrote to Kitsey, Mrs. Barbour, Hobie and Pippa.

To Kitsey, I explained that my death was not as a result of her and our situation at all. I thanked her for wearing my mother's earrings at our engagement party. To Hobie, I said that my death had nothing to do with all the bad pieces I'd sold and warned him that he would be hearing about them soon enough. I told Hobie a story of when I found a dog on the street. My mother refused, but finally relented to my fears. She agreed to take it home if it was still in the street after dinner.

Guess who was still on the street? Despite our best efforts, the dog died. This was my analogy of myself. The best for Hobie was for me to go. I thought, then, that there was probably a better and shorter way to tell Hobie my story. My mind wandered to what I would wear on the bed for when they found me. I was sick again in the bathroom, this time from illness, like the flu. I could hear visitors in the hotel coming in and going out for celebrations.

4

Just after my mother died, when I was a boy, I would try to keep the memory of her alive so I could dream about her. She never stayed. As an adult I would imagine that she lived across town and I just hadn't gone to see her for years, for some unknown reason. Finally, she came to me in my dreams. It was a gift to see her there. As she was about to speak, I woke up.

5

It was morning when I opened my eyes. I still felt my mother's presence in the room. I tried to hang onto that feeling, but the ringing of the Christmas church bells broke my reverie. Carefully, I got up and came to a conclusion. I took a shower and cleaned myself up. I would need to figure out a way to get Gyuri back his watch and ring. I had decided to turn myself in at the American consulate. I still needed to write letters, but instead of goodbye letters, they needed to be more of an explanation or declaration that I was would be gone for a while.

As I went to leave, I noticed a bag of candy that had been left on my door for the holiday. It reminded me that breakfast might not be too bad before I went. An hour later, a young teenager brought my holiday breakfast. I'd just sat down to enjoy some coffee when my room phone rang. It was the desk clerk letting me know that someone was on his way up, without being allowed.

I asked if he'd given a name, but no one had been around long enough to get that from him. I'd spilled coffee on myself from the surprise of the phone and began to worry that it was one of Martin's guys. My relief was great when I opened the door to see Boris. I explained to the hotel employee that it was okay.

I was surprised and wasn't sure about letting Boris in. He asked if I had somewhere to go and I said I did. As usual, Boris began to talk and talk about what he'd been doing. He was hungry and thirsty. He already helped himself to my champagne and juice as he kept talking. I gave him Gyuri's watch and ring, but he said I could give them back myself. I said I'd rather he did it. He suggested that we call him and order for more food. I wasn't in the mood for Boris and wanted to continue with my plan. He said there was a lot to tell. I got ready to go. Boris stopped me and told his story. I didn't want to hear it.

He had been sick, too, and had finally recovered. He and Gyuri had gone to Frankfurt. I interrupted him, asking for my passport. He passed it to me, still unwavering in his desire to finish his tale. He noticed that I was blank and we began to banter back and forth about when we were young. Boris asked why I hadn't read his texts. He looked at the ground at a bag he'd brought with him. I picked up the bag and started to leave when Boris told me to wait, wondering if I was going to open it. I had already learned my lesson about keeping the painting a secret, I knew what I had to do as I started for the door.

Boris stopped me and told me that it wasn't at all what I thought. He said it was better than anything I could think of. He told me to open the bag to see. There, I saw bricks of hundreds of dollars. Boris said that was only a fraction of the amount due to me. He said he would set up a Swiss account for me to get the rest. I didn't want anything to do with the money. I thought was all blood related, but Boris was offended.

I asked him to explain himself. I didn't want money; I wanted the painting. I thought he'd sold it and that was where the money came from. He explained that the idea had been mine. The money was reward money.

The art crimes division offers money for any information that leads to the recovery of paintings, all in cash. I had my doubts about what he was saying.

Boris got the man who owned the garage where we'd parked the car to call the cops and tell them where we thought some paintings might be held. Since there was no way that Boris was going to be able to get to the place where Sascha's old girlfriend lived and the place thought to be their hideout, they stalked the place, first to see if the Asian boy had shown up there.

They made up a story and called the cops, saying they thought a painting was held at that address. The best part of it was that there were two dozen or more stolen paintings there, and the reward money had been paid out for each piece. Sascha was caught and put in jail. His Asian boyfriend disappeared, never to be seen again.

Boris said that if he'd known how easy it was to get money from the US government by doing this kind of thing, he would have gotten into that much sooner. Furthermore, Horst claimed that he didn't know it was us that he'd sent his men after. If he had, it never would have happened, but Boris no longer trusted him.

With this news, I was speechless. I told Boris he needed to take some of the money, but he claimed to have taken his share of things, already. Plus, he said he felt so bad about how things went that he was happy to be able to make something right again. He tried to make an analogy to Dostoevsky's *The Idiot*. He suggested that sometimes good comes out of bad or that our mistakes can end up setting things straight again. He said that maybe everything happened for a reason. I realized that one of the reasons I'd always been drawn to Boris was that he was never afraid. It was rare to meet someone like that.

Boris asked where I'd been headed and suggested I stay a bit longer. I said I was going home. He convinced me to stay a couple of days in Antwerp with him.

6

I flew home two days later, arriving in the morning back at Hobie's place. He was troubled, but tried to pretend he was fine. We wished each other a Merry Christmas and tried to carry on conversation, but I knew something was wrong. Finally, I asked him what was going on.

First, he was quite upset with the necklace I'd left for Pippa. It had upset her as well. Then, Lucius Reeve had paid him a visit two days before Christmas and told him everything. Hobie wanted to leave the matter, but returned to it. He was upset by the whole thing. He was shocked that two million dollars worth of fake furniture that he'd restored was out there. He kept talking as I tried to calm him. I tried to tell him that I could pay it all back now and that I just hadn't known what to do and didn't know how to stop. Finally, Hobie asked me why I went to Amsterdam. He heard about the paintings and wanted to know why I'd come back. He thought I'd left for good. He was getting more and more upset. I told him I could explain, and he asked me to do so. I told him to sit down because it was a long story and I would do my best to make it short.

7

He didn't say a thing while I told him everything. When I finished, he sat in silence. Then, he said, "It does all swing around strangely sometimes, doesn't it?" I didn't know what that meant and he said he understood better as he got older. Suddenly, he stood up and I told him I would go. I said I would write him a check for the amount owed and would leave. He said not to, that he wanted to show me something. Returning from the parlor, he had with him an old photo album. As he leafed through it, he pointed to a faded snapshot. In it was a young boy. Next to a Manet was a replica of the very same painting that had haunted my life. It had captured Hobie's heart his whole life too. When Welty had taken Pippa to the museum, it was for the purpose of seeing that painting.

Hobie cleared his throat and asked how I had kept it stored. I told him in a cotton pillowcase and that I hadn't known any better. He said I could have told him about it. I thought that was true, but with everything else in my life at the time, it hadn't seemed feasible. He said he would have figured out something to help me. Then, he admitted that when I'd shown up from Vegas, it made everyone nervous. He still felt that it was Welty sending me to him for a reason. He said it reminded him of his own childhood where he'd wandered around after his mother's death until he came upon Mrs. De Peyster, who took him in.

Hobie commented that people don't really need all the things they have and it wasn't like it was helping society. He understood that when a painting touches you, it changes you.

8

My dad used to say, "sometimes you have to lose to win." Almost a year has passed since that day and I've spent most of it traveling. I've been going around the country, trying to retrieve the fake pieces and pay back the buyers. It's been good for me to be alone and to come to terms with my life in my own way. I've been led to a number of unique places in my search to recover the frauds. I feel different, and I'm different in my travels. It's a good feeling to move from place to place.

I've come to understand a great sorrow, that we don't get to choose our own hearts. We don't get to choose the people we are. It comes from our childhood and our culture. We're told to be ourselves and follow our hearts, but what if our hearts can't be trusted?

Maybe Kitsey is on to something. Maybe we should set our lives on a path that takes us towards the norm. Or maybe we should be like Boris, and just go head first through life. My engagement to Kitsey isn't off. I'm just not bound to honor the promise. It's a good feeling, really. When I'm in town, we get together and act like family, but that's all that's expected. Mrs. Barbour has gone out of the apartment a few times, now.

Pippa took the book, but left the necklace, saying she couldn't keep it, even though only I would have been able to pick such a beautiful gift for her. She said that I shouldn't think that she didn't love me, only that we were too much alike. Our bond over tragedy was too much for us to be together. She said there was no way that we would be good for each other. As you've read my story, you know that was never a worry. I could be the strong one. I could have been the one to keep us together.

In fact, my purpose in writing this whole story is that one day Pippa will read it and understand. I know this won't happen but it's still my hope. I guess I've been writing for a number of years, with notes of learning the business of antique dealing and my feelings upon returning to New York. If our secrets define us, then the painting was the secret that brought me above life and helped me to find myself. The painting was there amidst all of my writing, even though it's not there, directly.

We might even wonder what the painting meant to the painter, himself. It's such a simple painting, yet what kind of meaning did it hold? There's not enough of his work to know the answer. We can only wonder.

Throughout, there must be some truth about suffering to be learned. What if that goldfinch hadn't been captured, to become the subject of Fabritius' painting? Despite captivity, the bird is represented with dignity. There must be meaning within the imagery. I've come to understand that life is a catastrophe, no matter how much anyone says that it's wonderful and rewarding. Every move we make is a catastrophe.

Perhaps there is no point in suggesting that everything ends badly for us, even for the most hopeful and happy. Perhaps it's possible to suggest that to play in the game of life can bring a kind of joy of its own. I have written this story to try to understand the meaning of all things, even if it's not possible. On some level, I don't really want to understand, but I marvel at what the future might bring. I've been on the road so long that I dream of a journey and of snakes. They seem to remind me of Amsterdam and the period of time when I changed.

It was like the conversation I had with Boris about giving up the dope. He claimed that he had no problem stopping the drugs, but that there was nothing he could change about being an alcoholic. I asked why he didn't just stop if he wanted to. He said, "Live by the sword, die by the sword." In a way I understood. Sometimes, we can't help but want something, even if we know it will be the death of us. We cannot escape who we are.

I have come to understand that there's no truth beyond illusion. Art and magic exist in an *in between* state of reality and imagination. Even love dangles in that in between state. Pippa emanates this so well. The reality of our love is there, but the illusion of it ever coming to anything makes the *in between* a beautiful place to enjoy a promise of what can never be. For this reason I write. This is where the truth and the untruth come out. This is what has helped me to accept what's to come.

Life is like the love for the painting. For all the disaster that's come, so also has love. Whatever part we play in the existence of love adds to its history. My love for the painting joins the long line of people who have also loved it. It's this shared love that keeps us going from one generation to the next.

Final Recap

Donna Tartt has created a beautifully complex story of love showing an appreciation for art on many levels. *The Goldfinch* is a story about love: love for a mother, love for a father figure, love for a girl, love for a friend, and most importantly, love for a painting.

The story begins with the main character, Theo Decker, recovering from sickness in an Amsterdam hotel. He then takes us back to when his life completely changed with the loss of his mother and the gift of a painting that would change his life forever. Theo struggles through his teens as he deals with his mother's death and his father's gambling ways and eventual death.

Orphaned and lost, Theo finds comfort in the home of an antique dealer, the partner of the man he'd spoken to during his last moments on earth, where he'd been given Fabritius' famous painting, *The Goldfinch*. Theo's life is overshadowed by the painting until certain events change that and he realizes that he must be someone different or some other version of the person he might have been, had he never known the painting.

Critical Review

Donna Tartt's newest novel was received with high expectations, based on her past highly reviewed novels. For the most part, critics approved of the third. Vanity Fair says, *"Throughout these near 800 pages, we are reminded again and again of Donna Tartt's deep intelligence, for this is a bildungsroman that is intimately aware of its bildungsroman pedigree."*

The Guardian further praises, *"Plot and character and fine prose can take you far – but a novel this good makes you want to go even further."*

A rare negative review can be found. The Observer, laments an issue which is minimized in our summary, that, *"Conversations, monologues – many of them in Boris' broken and extremely tedious-to-read Russian accent – are drawn out over pages."*

Tartt has continued to impress with her talent for writing and weaving a complicated story that engages readers page by page.

If you enjoyed The Goldfinch in A Brief Read, maybe you can work in some time to read the original. If there's a book that you'd like to see in A Brief Read, let us know!

Visit us on Amazon or ABriefRead.com!

Like us on Facebook for special promotions!

CPSIA information can be obtained at www.ICGtesting.com
Printed in the USA
LVOW05s2306240414

383196LV00009B/311/P